ISBN: 978-1-4269-3861-0 (sc)
ISBN: 978-1-4269-3862-7 (e)

*Our mission is to efficiently provide the world's finest, most comprehensive
book publishing service, enabling every author to experience success.
To find out how to publish your book, your way, and have it available
worldwide, visit us online at www.trafford.com*

Trafford rev. 8/3/2010

 www.trafford.com

North America & international
toll-free: 1 888 232 4444 (USA & Canada)
phone: 250 383 6864 ◆ fax: 812 355 4082

A Day in the Sun

WRITTEN BY
Norman W. McGuire

1

The sun came up with the crack of the plow. Yes, it was going to be another great day. There was a slow dripping sound of water that came from the far side of the well house which meant the pump was leaking again. The birds were starting to flutter about in the trees and sing there morning song. The air still had that cool soft feeling that comes to the Oklahoma sunrise, and with it the smells of black ;jack, Johnson grass, salt grass, cats claw and the over laying smell of blue jumper, with some purple sage mixed in with it. The boy turned form the well house and walked down pass the milk house and out house, went over the fence onto the old' South forty. He looked about and thought "what a great day God has given to me, just makes a body want to sing, and what a great day to hunt old' Ben. Old' Ben was a large water moccasin that lived down by Frank Busshiehead'spond. The pond was in the middle of a wheat field there were a few trees, and a cattle guard you had to cross to get there. It was a good place to play except you had to look out for that snake, and he (the snake) wasn't shy about biting. The boy hated Ben. The snake had killed his best friend Tom blue stone just a month past, and the boy had made up his mind before the month was out he would count coop on the darn thing or know the reason why. The boy got himself a stick with a good reach, and then he took his knife and cut a sharp point at one end. "This will get him," thought the boy, and continued to make the end as sharp as a spear. While this was going on, old' Ben had decided to sun himself. He crawled out on a rock where the warm morning sun could warm him. He crawled his full length all of six feet, and lay flat. Yes it was going to be a good day, warm and quiet; he might even catch a mouse if he was lucky. He was content with the fact that he was safe; after all he was the biggest snake in three counties. The boy walked into the morning with his pointed stick, knife, baggy pants. No shirt, and his moccasins and his will, "sure" he thought, "The snake could kill him, but then he could also kill the snake." With this in mind he decided to be extra careful. Ben was just starting to feel warm after a long cold night, and the sunshine felt good when he felt the vibrations of someone walking. Well it was not a cow, or a dog, or horse, no this was smaller, and from the stride could only be a two legged creature. Well... he wasn't worried, he had already killed one two legged creature, a cow and several chickens this past spring, he could do it again, he went back to sleep. The boy was about twenty-five feet from the water hole, when he got down on his hands and knees, and started to crawl toward it. Ever few feet he would stop and search the ground in front of him. He was looking for the snake, and sure wanted to see him first. There he was.Damn, he was bigger then he had first thought, the boy almost turned around and run, but then he thought of his friend and how he died, and his resolve to kill the snake came back stronger then ever. Ben rolled his eyes toward the sky, it was going to be another warm July day, and he had a full summer to look forward to when, WHACK, WHACK, WHACK, the snake coiled to strike, where was that hitting coming from, he tried to get his wits and form a tight coil to protect his head, but the thing just wouldn't let up. Out of the side of his left eye he caught the movement of blue and brown, and the thing was jumping all around and yelling to beat the band, now the snake had had enough, as fast as the eye could wink, he coiled and drew back his head, picked his spot about half way up the blue and was in the process of striking when the lights went out. Ben was know more. He made the mistake of showing his head, and that was all it took, the boy had nailed him right between the eyes with the sharp end of his club. The snake twisted and coiled, but knows matter how it fought; it was nailed to the end of the stick, and would never be free of it again. There you old bastered, guess you won't be killing any more people or for that matter anything else again. Yes...it was going to be another good day, and the boy set off toward the house to get his breakfast, killing snakes this early sure gave a body a good appetite.

It was now the second week of July and the boy had stayed out of trouble for two whole days. Things just had to change. That morning his aunt had come back from Talaquah.and she had brought him a gift. It was a real tomahawk. Man, just what he needed. Now for about the last two months the boy had been making war on a robin. Or rather the robin had been making war on him. The bird would wait till the boy wasn't looking and then swoop down and pull his hair or drop some bird shit on him. It was down right disgraceful the way that made a body feel. Bad enough to be pecked, but to be shit on was the last straw. The boy had been raised on stories of how the Cherokee Indians had been the best at tomahawk fighting. He could just see himself with his tomahawk setting out

3

on the trail of a bear or deer, and with one swing, cutting the animal down, and then bringing it home and showing it off. The boy waited all morning for his aunt to get home and give him the gift. At last about noon he saw her car turn into the long driveway and start up to the house. He was at the car door before she had even stopped the car. Where is it? Where is it? He asked. Right here, just hold your horses for crying out loud. The aunt reached into the bag at her side and pulled out a tomahawk. The handle was about 18 inches long and it had a steel head. It felt good in his hands. Now don't be killing any thing with it, it is just to be put in your room for show. You got that.Yeah.I got it. only what the boy meant when he said he got it and the way she took it was two different things. The boy cut out for the orcnerd. This was the one place he could go to and be alone with his thoughts or what ever. It wasn't really a orchard, it was just a bunch of trees that had been planted some time in the late 20's or 30's.some one said the W.P.A.was the ones who put them in but know one really knew for sure. The boy didn't care who put them in, it was his place to get away from the world, and have some peace of mind and just take a load off. The tree that the boy selected was a dead post oak. It had died the death of a lightning strike. The boy went over and marked out an -x- on the tree. He backed up about twenty feet, and began to practice. At first he couldn't even hit the tree. But after a few hours of practice, he was able to hit the tree and after a few more he was able to hit the mark. To stick a tomahawk took a lot of practice. The boy was certain that the Cherokee men who had been so skilled at it were just wizards in discuses as men. But he learned after a time that it took a lot of work to be able to stick a tomahawk where you wanted it to. He worked till the sun went down. Then he heard his grandma calling him to supper, well he thought, at least I can hit the tree and make it stick at least three out of four times, maybe I can do better tomorrow. With that last thought, he turned toward the house, but his resolve was not to say anything to his grandparents, cause if he did there would be no end to there nagging.

The next day was a Tuesday, and what a day. This was the day his grandpa went to see old man Push Feather. His grandma would be down at the spring talking with all the other women, it would be a perfect day to do what he wanted to do. Kill THAT RED BREASTED BASTERED.!!!!!!!!. Yes, he would do it to day. Ok, so maybe he was not too good with the tomahawk, well he would trust to luck.

The boy went down and ate a few bits of bacon, and biskets, then he got out his tomahawk and started to sharpen it. He wanted a razor edge on it when the time came. Soon he heard the shit dropper sing out, that is what he called it. The shit dropper, so he took up the weapon and out he went to do battle. Coming out the side door to the house he saw it. There it set in its entire splendor, on the side of the elm tree just singing its heart out. The boy took careful aim. And let fly. The throw was good, but it missed the tree and went on about ten feet and took his grandpa's Best coonhound in the head. The dog died a graceful death. It just kicked two or three times and died. Uh oh, the boy said, and about that time he felt something land on his right shoulder. He tuned his head to the left and saw his grandpa looking at him with cold blue eyes. His grandpa was one of the few blue eyed Cherokee's. when you looked into his eyes it was like looking in to the depths of a cold blue pool of water, or into the dark blue of the early morning sky it depended on if he was mad or not. Right now he looked like he was ready to take a scalp. And it was his he was looking at.

His grandpa didn't say anything, he just kind of nudged the boy toward the hog pen. Oh well... thought the boy, I guess I am going to get old Ned for this, then he saw the tomahawk in his grandpa's hand, oh God!!! Is he going to kill me???, .No Bend over chch, that is what his grandpa called him, it meant boy in Cherokee, I have to correct you. Then the boy saw the tomahawk in his grandpa's hand. Oh damn is he going to cut off my head? Thought the boy, then he got his answer, whack on his butt went the flat side of the tomahawk, then whack,whack,whack, damn wasn't he ever going to quite.

Chch, all things must die, as that is the way the great God set things up, but it is wrong for you, or any man to help the God of all. To do this, you place you self in the place of being God, and that is wrong. This is what his grandpa said, then he gave the tomahawk back to the boy, and went to bury the dog The boy just stood there with tears coming down his cheeks, his butt was hurting, and he felt a kind' a slow anger building, not at his grandpa, but toward the bird. The boy never stopped to ask himself why he was mad at the bird, he only knew that he was, and that like it or not war had now come to the bird. It would be a war to the death, and the boy was going to do all in his power to take out the enemie.

The next afternoon the boy was out stalking the bird again. He had made up his mind that if he was going to kill the bird, it would have to be soon, cause once again the bird had dive bombed him that very morning, and he was getting tired of cleaning bird shit out of his hair. He thought to himself that in order to kill the pest he would have to get to the well house and glide to the barn yard. As he watched he realized that it was when feeding that the bird was less watchful. He also began to notice that the bird fed mostly in the morning and again in the afternoon.

With this knowledge, the boy went in to eat supper, tomorrow would be soon enough to get the thing that had been making his life so bad. Tomorrow, look lout, POW.

The boy was up before his grandpa, and had his tomahawk with him. He went down the stairs as quite as an owl in flight. He eased himself out the side door, and went around the cellar, down past the well house, under the fence, and into the barn yard. He found himself a place behind a bail of hay, and set down to wait. About thirty minutes went by, and he was getting tired of sitting in his cramped position when he heard the chirp of the robin. He looked over the top of the hay and saw the bird fighting a worm in a cow pie. The worm did not want to take wings for love or money, the bird on the other had was just as stubborn about the worm learning to fly, so it was a type of tug-o-war between worm and bird.

The boy raised the tomahawk and took good aim, drew back his hand and let fly. The tomahawk turned about three times in the air and as neat as you please took off the head of the bird. The head kept hanging on to the worm, and the worm was fighting to get back into the ground, and the bird's body was flopping all around much as a chicken did when his grandma cut off there heads for Sunday supper. The boy just stood and watched the whole thing as it took place in front of him. After a few minutes, the worm worked him self free and crawled back into his hole, the birds body quite doing its death dance, and all was quiet. The boy walked over to the bird and picked up the head and the body. He looked at the two parts and started to cry. I am sorry bird, I didn't mean to kill you, I just wanted you to quite dumping on me, I didn't mean to hurt you, please forgive me.

The boy buried the bird out behind the milk barn and started to walk back to the house, as he passed under the

Elm tree he heard a chirping sound. He stopped and looked up. He could just see a nest about halfway up the tree. He jumped and started to climb the tree. When he reached the nest, he looked over the edge and there he saw two little robin babies. Oh man, thought the boy what will you do without your mamma? The he hit upon a great idea, he could be there mom. Yeah..., that would work, he could get worms, and bugs and give them to the young.

The boy spent the rest of the next three weeks digging worms and tracking down grasshoppers to feed the young robins, and his grandparents never knew he was doing it, at all though they did wonder at the boys actions of digging up ever worm he could find, and chasing down all the hoppers he could catch, then climbing the tree with them. At first his grandparents thought he was going to play a joke on them by dropping them down on there heads as they walked under the tree, but soon gave up that idea. Then they thought he was eating them because it seemed to them his appetite had fell off. But after three weeks he started to eat again, and act like his old self, so they soon forgot all about it.

Truth was the boy quite eating because he was sick all the time. You see catching the worms and the bugs was only half the feeding of the birds. He then had to crush them all together, and that was the part that turned his stomach. Oh... it wasn't the crushing of the bugs that got to him, it was the feeding of them to the birds. Just the thought of swallowing anything that looked and smelled that bad just turned your gut into a ball. To say the least, the boy never killed another robin. Just the idea of feeding the family after word was more then he could bear. Many the time after he had killed the robin he had wished that he had just let the bird shit all over him, it was a darn sight easier to get clean, then feed a pack of starving young.

2

This is the first day of the rest of your life that is what the sign said that hung from the side of the dirty little one room gas station off old route 66. The boy stood there a moment and thought about the words and what they meant. Who ever wrote this was a deep thinker, thought the boy. I better not tell grandpa what I read though, cause then he would think I was putting on airs, and that just wouldn't do, and I don't want to get into any more trouble for awhile, after all its only about two weeks scence I killed his coon dog, I don't need any more problems on my plate right now.

He set off down the dusty country road, kicking up small puffs of red dust with his bear feet. He was humming a song that he heard his uncle sing. His grandpa said that the words were nasty, and he must never speak them, but if he only hummed the tune and didn't sing the words he didn't think that would be a sin. The meadow larks were singing at the top of the beak power, that is what the boy side birds did to make noise, beak power, and the grass hoppers were counting grass blades and talking about it, the June bugs were not as yet, and the wind was soft and warm as it usually gets in late July in Oklahoma. The boy didn't have a care in the world, and that is what bothered him, because when ever he felt like this it usually meant he was in for a rough squall. Well he would face that when it came but it seemed to him life would be a lot better if a person could keep a little trouble handy, that way he wouldn't have to always be on the lookout for the hard stuff, cause when trouble went looking for a place to lit, if it saw you already had some it would just go in and leave you alone, but if it saw you were free of any at the time it would just jump all over you, and when it got done, you felt like you had been hit by a train, or to use the boys own words, a steamer.

While the boy was walking home his grandma had made a rude discovery. Some critter had broke into her chicken house and had killed about 4 or 5 of her chickens, and from the looks of it old' red was back in town. Now old' red was a fox, and not your regular garden variety type of fox. He was a chicken stealing, crap smearing, wire cutting, egg eating, piss in the corner, bad tempered type of fox. This was the boy's grandma's description of old' red. The boy often wondered how such a genteel type woman, and God fearing to boot, could become so worked up over a critter like old' red.

As the boy was walking up into the yard he saw his grandma come kitting around the milk barn, run between the garden and the well house, past the cellar and into the house. Now just what in thunder is going on now, thought the boy ? I knew it was to quite around here, and the boy swore latter that it sounded just like a banker with a splinter in his butt. Now for a splinter to be in a regular persons butt was one thing, but to be in a bankers butt was just awful. Everyone knew that the only way a banker made his living was by sitting on there butts and figuring out how to trick the people out of there hard won money, so a splinter there would be about like breaking a working mans fingers, cause a working man made his way in life with his hands, and a banker made his way sitting down, being rude and, just put a banker out to pasture for sure. When ever some one said they had a pain in the ass, they usually meant banking troubles.

The boy was thinking this when his grandma came around the side of the house lugging his grandpas shot gun. Oh Lord, groaned the boy, she's going to shoot me for sure. Ger your self over here and give me a hand, shouted his grandma. I got a critter to lay out and time is waisten. A critter the boy asked?. Yes a critter, and he has long red hair and a sharp skinny nose. Old' red shouted the boy. Yes old' red it is, and I ain't going to let the sun set till I have him. How are you going to catch him, asked the boy?. I aint going to catch him darn your hide, I am going to kill, skin and fry his him. Now come here . I want you to put your nose to the ground and sniff him out for me. You know where ever critter in three counties live, and I mean to have him, now get to it , and play like a good dog and I might let you live to see another sunrise.

The boy turned around and started down toward the road. Hey where you going, shouted his grandma? The deed was done down at the chicken house, I would think that is the place to start looking. The boy changed directions and headed toward the chicken house. He looked around some and found the tracks of the fox. Well where do you want me to start? I found the tracks and they lead off toward the hog pen. Well don't look at me retorted his grandma, I don't have no tracks on me, there on the ground, so you just put your nose there and follow it, I wont be far behind. That was what the boy was afraid of. The thought of a load of bird shot in the ass made his mind foggy. If she did shoot him he would have to stand up a pizin long time and that reminded him of the time him and his cousin burnt down the outhouse. How was they to know that the grape vines would burn so long.. Man it made a heck of a fire. His grandpa said it was because it was human shit that did it. He said cow shit would burn hot and put off a Puget smell, horse shit burnt fast and made no flame, but human shit just burnt up everything. There was a loud explosion that came from the outhouse, and his grandpa said it was shit gas, so from then on the boy was careful not to eat much in the way of beans or cabbage, cause ever one knew that they caused gas, and the boy didn't cotton to much to the idea of sitting down to go and the next thing finding himself sitting on the roof of the house.

Get with it shouted grandma, this was what shook him out of his current thoughts. He looked around and saw his grandma coming up behind him and damn if she didn't have that gun pointed straight up his backside. Kind of made you a little quizzey in the gut. The last time old' red had come by his grandma had shot up the whole farm. She had put holes in the milk house, barn, well house and one through the roof of the house. She put that one there when she was cleaning the gun, so she said that one didn't count, but to the boy's way of thinking a shot that counted or didn't count didn't matter if it hit you.

Putting the threat of a shot up the ass behind him, the boy pressed on, and kept to the trail of the fox. He found that the trail lead around the side of the chicken house and down toward the hog pen. He stuck with the trail, and it was pretty easy to follow due to the fact that the fox kept dropping chicken feathers ever so may feet. All the boy had to do was follow the feather trail. Soon he found where the fox had dropped the chicken and had eaten a little, then had picked it back up and went on. The boy stopped when the trail crossed over the dirt country road. What you stopping for asked his grandma?. Well he crossed over the road and into redsong's field. Well what of it, if you don't move along I'll plug you, and you don't want that do you? What about the High Sheriff? You let me worry about the sheriff, and ol'walt too, now do like I said and get along with you, and I mean now.

The boy turned around and crossed his fingers, and said a fast prayer, and while he was at it asked a special blessing for his butt. The idea of having more then one whole back there was almost more the he could stand.

The fox ran a crisis-cross trail up through the blackjack's and sage brush, but the boy stuck to it for all he was worth, and grandma stuck to the boy with a prod form the gun if she felt he was slowing down any. The boy didn't want to say anything to her about it, because when she was having one of these types of fits, she was more likely to shoot then not. The trail took a turn back toward the road and the boy stopped, and looked around. His grandma stopped next to him and asked why he was stopping? Well said the boy, it looks like he is heading for the berry patch. His grandma looked where the boy was looking and had to agree. She asked, do you think he is in there? Well I can't say for sure. But if he is he will run out the other side as soon as we walk in. That's true, that's true, said his grandma, tell what you count to a slow 100 and that will give me time to get around to the other side. When you reach 100 you start to walk in, and I'll lay low, when he comes out it will be like new hay, I'll plug him and then we can be finished with this business. She sidled off to the right, and began to circle. The boy started his slow count. It seem like it took him for ever to reach 100 but after a few years he made it. He then started to walk into the bushes. There came a rustling in front of him, and he saw the swish of a red bushy tail, and then he heard the loud crack, or more like a boom of the shot gun. The boy was to forever question his eyes on what he saw next, but to put it in his own words it went something like this, first thing you know this critter came up out of those berries just like a frog on a hot plate, next thing he did was to just jump around on his hind legs with his head back and kind of grinned at the sky, then he did a kind of one paw cartwheel and the last I saw o him he was scooting down the road and gaining ground ever time his feet hit. It was latter found out that the gun had been loaded with rock salt to keep the peskies out of the water melon patch, and his grandpa had forgot to reload with lead shot. The boy was forever convinced that a load of rock salt in the rear was a sure fire way to get a person up and moving, at least it worked on fox's.

3

Well the fox lit out of the country, and grandma found a small part of it's fur hanging from a bramble, and took it home and put it between two pages of the family bible like she did everything else she wanted to save, and by the time she had told the story twenty or thirty times and embellished on it and worked it over to her satisfaction you would of thought that she had killed a whole heard of fox's and single handed saved ever chicken in the state of Oklahoma not to mention the whole darn United States of America. The Indian noble ladies club gave her the good citizen ship award for the quarter and she even had her picture in the paper. Yep, to use the boys words, grandma really spread her self out, and didn't pull any punches doing it.

A week or so went by and things had kind of cooled down, and there didn't seem to be any more exciting times in the near future. The boy had settled into a kind of routine. Get up, wash, eat, go out to the garden and weed the patch as he called it, come in at noon and eat again, then knock off for the rest of the day and go fishing, or mooning around the milk barn looking for rats that he might kill, or down to the orchard and see what kind of trouble was going on there, or sit out by the mail box and wait on the post to run. To say the least he was bored out of his mind. In a latter time he would be grateful for this time, and had he only know what was coming down the road at time he would have enjoyed it more then he did.

About seven days after the great fox hunt, a black car pulled off the dusty county road and rolled down the drive way and stopped in front of the house. A man got out, and taking a large trunk from the back seat walked up to the door. The car then turned and drove back the way it had come. The boy was down at the hay barn and from the loft saw the whole thing. Well says he, this is new hay, someone come calling, hanging down in front of the loft door he slid down the rope to the ground, and started up to the house.

He was just coming up to the door when he heard his grandma sing out John. John, Hugh thought the boy, I wonder if this is that uncle that I keep hearing about, the one that is supposed to be a preacher?. He bent his head toward the door so he could hear better. Eddie, John said I wouldn't of known you if it was not for all that hair, my but you have put on some weight. Well John, I see you haven't changed any, still as low browed as ever, well what are you doing here ?. I came to stay a while. I lost my church when I started to talk again drinking, smoking, and snuff dipping, and chewing, and all that sort of rot, so the folks just kind of asked me to shove. So here I am, can you put me up for awhile ?. Well I reckon, but it does put a squeeze on us to do it, but well get by some how. The boy continued to listen, but the conversation was moving back into the house and he couldn't pick up any more of it.

Well if that don't beat all, he just shows up out of know where and moves right in and makes himself at home. If the boy only knew how much at home his uncle was to make himself he would have split clean out of the country, but that is latter on, so lets just worry about this one thing at a time.

It was supper when the boy was to have his first idea that things had changed, and it looked like it would be sometime till the storm blew over. The boy as was his custom set right down and started to dig in when crack, he got a hard wood spoon across his knuckled, and a loud voice that said wait till the blessing has been asked. Asked hell, he thought, I was just doing what I always do, and this jar-head is telling me to hold off, what is going on any way. The uncle bowed his head and folded his hands, and started to grumble over the food. The boy looked first at his grandma, then at his grandpa and saw that they were doing the same thing, well if they could do it so could he, so he bowed his head and folded his hands and waited till his uncle got done complaining about the food, and only when he finished with a big flourish and a loud AMEN, did the boy look up, and when he did he found himself looking into the coldest set of black eyes he was to ever see.

This is your uncle John, his grandma said in the way of an introduction and John this is Pats boy. Now what do you say to your uncle, come on don't be shy. The boy looked up at his uncle and still feeling the smart on his hand from the spoon said, you hit me again with me not looking and your going to wish you never came here, the boy got a slap across his mouth from his dear ol'uncle, who then said, manners are something to be learned, and that such a undisciplined boy would have to come to terms or else The boy didn't want to know what the terms were, but felt that they would put a damper on any fun he might have in the near future, or for that matter the rest of his life. The boy set in abject silence for the rest of the meal, and made a swift retreat as soon as the plates were picked up. It did him no good.

Boy come down here, his uncle called, I have something for you to do. The boy came down the stairs as slowly as he could. Yes he asked , what do you want ? You will not take that tone of voice with me, his uncle said, and then clouted him up the side of the head. Hey...why did you do that, the boy asked, I only answered you question. I will tolerate no form of malice from one so young in years as your self. Now get over here for your nightly bible reading. We will endeavor to do this ever night and twice on Sunday. Oh God thought the boy, my easy life is over, and I'll never again be free to be my self. Religion had come to roost on the boy's house.

They read the first few chapters in the book of Matthew, and then his uncle said a pizzen long prayer, where he asked blessing on ever thing from having good crops to people he didn't even know, and kept calling out name's like, you know who and old so and so, and kept it up till the boys knees went to sleep and he had to helped up off the floor when the thing was all said and done. The boy took to calling these nightly intrusions on his knees as the time of bored pain. He tried to miss them when ever he could, but know matter how late he stayed out, or how ever soon he went to bed, is uncle would always roust him out, or hunt him down to go through the business, and it seemed to the boy that the prayers got longer and windier by the night, till he thought that some night they would all kneel down to pray and go right on through to the next day might even meet there own self's fixing to kneel down again. This got him worked up into such a sweat that he started looking for way's to leave the house in case it happened. Time seemed to stand still for the boy for the next two weeks, and it seemed all he did was dodge his uncle, or pray. Now the boy had his own form of religion, and it went something like this, you always treat ever one the way you want to be treated. Never steal, cause if you did some one might come along and just clean you out. Never take God's name in vain. He didn't know what God's name was, but decided that the word GOD was good enough. Never treat an animal mean, cause they were dumb and could not be held responsible for there action's. Don't ever lie, cause ever one knew if you told a lie the devil would move into your mouth and take up house keeping and the boy just couldn't cotton to that know way. His religion was honest. And simple. He had a great love for God and all that God had created. He had not got this in a church, but from watching the ever day actions of God at work on the farm Seeing the baby calf come into the world, or watching a mother hen watch over her chicks, or the way a hawk rose and fell with the wind, or how the plants came up from the ground after a good rain, and then covered with the warm sun. No, the boy's religion was pure, and simple, but this jack leg uncle was trying to change all that and the boy was not about to let that happen, after all it was his grandpa who told him God was in how you saw him, not how some one made him out to be. The boy could live with that.

It was on the second Sunday after Uncle John came to live with them that he turned the whole house out to have sunrise prayer. Something had to be done about this nonsense. Even his grandpa said things had gone to far, and that praying was ok at the eating table , but that the cows had to be milked and sure couldn't do it down on his knees in the front yard for the first hour after sun came up. To the reader let it be known that cows have to be milked about the same time ever morning and afternoon or the utters (tits) will swell and in some cases even quite giving milk, and if you dairy farm this is trouble in the worst way, so his grandpa felt it his duty to say something to uncle John about the new sunrise ceremonies that his uncle had decided that the family needed to keep them on the right path. The talk didn't go to well, but then again maybe it was the way his grandpa came about doing it It was Monday morning when the uncle turned every one out to do there ceremonies when his grandpa said to John, now see here John, this has gone about far enough, I can see praying over the vitals, and even before going to bed, but this morning business is a bit to much. I got cows to milk, and feed, and hogs to slop, and chickens to feed and Lord knows what all else that comes up through the day, and I can't be spending time down here jawing on my knees when I got so blame much work to do. Now I tell you what I'll do, being as the ceremonies are so important to you, I'll go along with them if, when were done, you'll come along down and lend me and the boy a hand with all the other stuff. Uncle John didn't say anything, but the boy noticed that there were no more sunrise ceremonies after the talk. You see when the Morning Prayer was over and everyone else went to work, Uncle went back to bed. The boy use to say his uncle was hell on wheels to pray, but was as limp as a fish tail when it came to working for a living. From then on the boy lumped lazy preachers in with the bankers and politician's of his day. To him they were all the same, useless.

Once the morning ceremonies were stopped, his uncle set into him even worse. Even his grandpa and grandma said something about it, so when ever they were around his uncle would act nice, and do right, but the minute there back were turned then he would set into the boy with a vengeance that was so much like war that the boy felt like he had done battle with the best of them and at the least should be given some kind of meddle.

The day came when the boy could take know more. All his jeans had there knees wore out, and he was starting to get calluses on his knees, and had about wore out his hands from folding them so much that he was scared that some day he would get down on his knees and fold his hands and be stuck like that for the rest of his life, something had to be done and fast, but what...?

It was on the second Monday of August when the boy was down in his orchard, and was worrying over the problem like a dog does a bone when a plan began to take place, and the more he thought about it the better it got, now if he could pull this off he would have his uncle out of his hair, not to mention the house and the sooner the better Almost two days latter as the boy was trying to sleep in his lofty perch in the attic, he waken with a tolerable thirst. The dog days of August had set in and there just wasn't any cooling off even when the sun went down. His grandpa said it was like this once in the bible but he couldn't remember where it said it, but swore it was there. The boy could believe it, cause he sweat most as much at night as he did during the day, and it was getting so there just wasn't enough water to fill him up any more. He got out of bed and went down the stairs to get a drink. He had to go softly cause the stairs creaked and groaned so as to wake the dead, so he was moving real slow when he heard movement below him. Now who could be up moving about at this hour he thought ?.

He slowed his pace and waited to see who it was. He didn't have long to wait, for here come his uncle. Uncle John walked below the stirs and stopped, and looked about. Next he went on by into the kitchen and the boy lost sight of him. Moving on down the stairs, the boy looked around the corner into the kitchen and there was his uncle standing next to the sink and looking all about. Now what is he up to the boy wondered ?. His uncle stood real stiff for about the space of a minute, then stretched out his head on his skinny neck and looked all around, next he reached up and opened the door to the cabinet that contained the OLD CROW. The crow as the boy called it was pizzen bad whiskey. I mean it would boil your inside's till they were white, so the boy looked on in wonderment as his uncle took out the cork and pored himself about a whole water glass full. Now what in thunder is he doing that for, I mean with him being a preacher and all, he ain't got no right to be doing that and the boy started to say something, when a sudden thought stopped him he just stood back and watched. This was better then the plan he had.

His uncle held the whiskey up in front his eyes and looked at it, next he brought it down under his nose and sniffed it like a dog sniffing a tree, then he got this smile on his face like a cat with her mug in the cream and took a sip. He rolled it around in his mouth for a few seconds then he swallowed it down. He let out a small sound like AHHH, then proceeded to drink the whole thing down in one gulp. The boy watched in rapt attention. He knew he had his uncle, but how to use it...? He would think about that latter, for the moment he was just gloating in the fact that his psalm singing old bastered was about to get his, and that was all that counted.

The next day when his uncle sauté him out to do his bible reading the boy went about it with no fuss. At first his uncle was pleased, as he thought to him self that soon he would have this little whelp under his thumb, and there was nothing he liked better then to have the upper hand, but then he got to thinking that this was something new. This kid was not the kind to knuckle under so easy, so what was up...this was something he would have to think on. And because of these thoughts he lost his place in the reading and had to start all over.

The fact that his uncle for got where he was in the reading did not go unnoticed by the boy. In side he was shouting with joy, for he had learned a lesion about human behavior. If you act a certain way, people acted different. This was a new revelation to the boy. He was not sure but what he had learned was a valuable lesson. Well... he would just put this aside for now because he had an uncle to fry.

That night after ever one had gone to bed the boy went down the stairs again and went to the cabinet where the OLD CROW was kept. He took down the bottle and being careful not to spill a drop, poured the contents into a mason fruit jar, and then he poured turpentine and caster-oil into the whiskey bottle. Then he went back to his hiding place behind the stairs, and waited for his uncle to make his appearance. He did not have long to wait.

The clock was going on to one when the boy heard his uncle stirring around. He got as quite as the night crouched even lower and slowed his breathing down to almost nothing. His uncle appeared in the door way and looked about before going into the kitchen. The boy heard him open the cabinet and the sound of the bottle being put down on the table. Next he heard his uncle pull the cork and sound of liquid being poured out into the class. What happened next he could not be sure of, only what he could guess at, his uncle must have been in a hurry to get his nightly blessing cause he didn't stop to sniff it, he just gulped it down. The boy thought latter it must have been one heck of a surprise to his uncle when that mixture his gut, cause all the sudden there was the loudest sound as if a hair-lipped dog was loose in the kitchen. Sounded like Barffffffff... Then he heard the sound of breaking glass. And the sound of water running, he also heard his grandparents coming down the hall. When his grandpa came in to the room he had his shotgun pointed at what he thought was a robber, but then sees it's only John and lowered his gun down to his side. He looked around and saw the broken glass on the floor, and the whiskey bottle on the cabinet, then at Uncle John with his head in the sink running water in his mouth and all over his head, and face. His grandpa sings out "SOLD I reckon. Ma look what we got here now." His grandma came into the room and took the picture in, the she lets out a war-hoop and belts John in the gut. This folded him up like a fish worm on a hot rock. "Hey now, what you want to belt me for"?. John groaned. " I'll thank you to pack your grip and be out of my house before breakfast, cause if you ain't I'll take that shotgun and do to you what I did to a fox not long ago."

Uncle John was gone before breakfast. It was a little before noon when the boy was down at the milk house with his grandpa when his grandpa said " You know that drink John took last night was not like any he expected to get. I reckon the spirits in that bottle turned on him, cause when I went to put the bottle up I took a sniff of it, and it didn't smell like crow, no sir, but it did smell like caster oil and something else although I cant quite make it out. Now what do you suppose it was"?. He then turned and looked at the boy, but the boy couldn't meet his eye. His grandpa went on to say that that if a person be a drinker that sooner or later the spirits caught up with you and like it or not it would lay you out on a cold slab somewhere. Nothing more was ever mentioned about the crow, or uncle John and his midnight wondering in the house, how ever the boy did notice that the caster oil and the turpentine was put up and know matter how much he searched for it he never could find it. But ever now and then he would catch his grandparents looking at him and smiling, or if someone would mention drinking whey would say something like they had a sure fire cure for it, and then laugh real hard and look at him, which always made him uncomfterable, and wish he was 100 miles away.

The rest of the week passed uneventful except when grandma got into it with the general. The general was an old goose that lived down by the pond, and was the leader of about 15 or more geese, They never came up to the house, but always stayed down by the pond, but for some reason known only to the general they came to the garden one day and did battle with his grandma.

The boy was up in his perch in attic and saw the whole thing. Grandma was hoeing around her strawberries, and not bothering any one when here comes the geese. The general walked up behind grandma, and she never heard him. She was bent over working and the general stuck out his head and took a bill full of her rump. Grandma howled like a stuck pig and jumped and whirled around to see who had goosed her, thinking it was probably grandpa and low there was the goose. She turned a slow circle and saw that se was circled by geese. From where the boy set it looked like a big wheel, with grandma being the hub, and the geese the spokes. Grandma still had her hoe in her hand so she took a swipe at the geese to clear a path so she could get away and while she was swing at one goose another got a bill full of her leg. Grandma yells " I'll crucify the lot of yaw. " She then started to swing the hoe in front of her and took off running for the house. She only made it to the roof of the cellar.

The cellar roof stuck up about two and a half feet above the ground, and when grandma got there, being short and plump she was hard put to climb up, but the general gave her another goose and that seemed to help her some. As a matter of fact, after the general gave her some help by taking a hunk of her left cheek, she just sort of landed in the middle of the cellar roof. The geese being shorter of legs were having an even harder time trying to get to the roof Grandma was hopping mad by now. She still had her hoe so she lit in to them for all she was worth. She clouted one up the side of the head and killed him a grave yard dead. This seemed to set the others into a fit, and the general went into a white feathered fit. He honked and flapped his wings and the others started to do the same thing and then they all rushed the cellar at the same time. From where the boy set it was just old Ned. He said latter that what with his grandma hoeing geese necks and all the honking and wing flapping and the feathers flying around that it was better then the fourth of July.

The boy thought about going down and helping, but after watching the way grandma was swinging the hoe he thought better of it. She just might take him for a goose too and take off his head as well. No he would just stay put and watch and pay the punishment latter if he had to.

The battle lasted about thirty minutes or less, and when the feathers quite flying around there stood grandma with her hoe and still in charge of the roof, and all the geese were either dead or waking around with broke wings. Some of them had broken legs and were just laying about. The general was one of these. Grandma looked over the battle ground and then got down from the room. She walked around the battle field and surveyed her handy work. When she got to the general she stopped and looked at him. The general never gave an inch. He set there on the ground and held his head as high as he could and honked up a storm and looked her in the eye the whole time. Grandma brought the hoe back and with one fatale swing took his head off. "There Duran your hide, that will teach you to be a grabbing folks in places that don't belong to you." She then swung the hoe to her shoulder and set off for the tool shed.

While she was going to the tool shed grandpa was pulling into the yard on his wagon. He got down from the high seat and lead the team over to the water trough. He was standing there just looking around when he spied the geese. Well now...He thought, what in thunder nation had been going on now? He got has answer when grandma came around the corner of the shed and lit into him for keeping geese. She told him if he brought another goose on the place that she would collar him and tie him up and force him to live with them till the sky fell in. He tried to tell her that it was her idea to keep geese and that he never liked them any way, but she wasn't having any of that, and said he better listen to her or there would be trouble, so he shut up and she went back to the house to get the boy to start dressing the geese for the smoke house.

That evening as the boy and his grandpa set cleaning the geese his grandpa asked what had brought all this on, and the boy said that he didn't rightly know for sure, but that some how grandma had got cross ways of the general and the rest of the geese and that they had came up to the house looking for trouble, and when they got there that they had found it in bushels, and that grandma was hard put to save her hide but that she never backed down one bit, but went right into it with the geese and that from where he set it was just old' Ned to see the way grandma did battle with the geese, and his grandpa said he would of liked to of seen it cause it had been some time since he had seen a good fight, and the boy said he sure missed one this time, and grandpa said it wasn't fair the way he got left out of things and started to feel sorry for him self, but the boy said for him to cheer up that tomorrow was another day and maybe grandma hadn't killed all the geese and so there might be another fight then, so his grandpa perked up some and said he would wait and see.

Not much happened the rest of the week except that the boy had to keep the smoke house going, and was hard put to make sure that there was plenty of smoke and that the heat stayed pretty much the same, and after a while he started to smell like wood smoke so that when he walked through the house it smelled like something was on fire and his grandma said she was going to start following him around with a bucket of water just in case he lit up and he said it wasn't fair for him to have to keep the smoke house going when it was her that had been the one that had created the whole mess, and she thumped him on the head with her thimble and told him to hush his head, and that he would be grateful when it came time to eat the Duran things and he said he didn't want to eat the geese and that he didn't even like geese and she got mad and told him to do the job or she would smoke him along with the rest of the critters, so he shut up and went on, but was still hard put to like it and said so to his grandpa, and he said just do it, that there were times in life when you had to do jobs that weren't nice or fair but they had to be done, and the best way was just to do them and get it over with and be done with it. So the boy did, but vowed, that when he got older he would fight shy of jobs he didn't cotton to even if it killed him.

4

It was a couple of days after uncle John had pulled his freight, and the boy was down in the orchard sitting up in his favorite tree and was thinking over all the things that had gone on the last few weeks. He was stumped as to how so much could happen in such a short amount of time. Even his grandparents had talked about it. He had heard them just last night when they were sitting outside taking in the cool evening breeze. His grandpa has started it by saying "I never saw the beat of it. This summer has been one of the most mixed up, turned around times I can ever remember having. Just look at the way things has paned out would you?." What are you talking about now pa?". I don't see that this summer has been all that interesting, I mean not much more has gone on then usual." Well now...I wouldn't say that now ma, just take a look at that fox you bagged, and getting your picture in the paper, and then John showing up and causing all the ruckus, and disturbing ever body, I would say this past summer has been a real hum-dinger. I would." " You would , would you?" Well maybe your right, I just cant see it is all, but give me some time and maybe I will."

The boy thought it had been a pretty good summer up till he had heard them talking about it, but now he wasn't so sure. Well he would just wait and see what the rest of the summer had in store before he made up his mind to which way the wind was going to blow. For now he was at peace with him self, what with no uncle around to rag on him. And roust him out ever time he wanted to pray, and knock him around ever time he got upset about something. Yeah...life had come to him. And he guessed maybe that was just the way things went, when you thought you could take know more, trouble would let up and give you a breather. Well he was going to take it while it lasted, cause trouble might go away for awhile, but sooner or latter it would come calling at your door step and things would start all over again.

Getting down from his perch, he went toward the house, and was feeling all kind of happy and thinking that things was going to be all right, and was all wrapped up in himself when he felt the sting that just cut the flinders our of his ankle. Looking down he saw a coiled up and ready to strike again a rattler. The boy let out a whoop, and started making tracks for the house, As he ran he was yellowing snake bite at the to of his lungs, and thinking trouble came to him a whole lot faster then he thought.

By the time he had reached the house he had yellowed shake bite about 50 times and he looked up and say his grandpa coming out the side door, so changed directions and headed toward him. When he got there he fell into his grandpa's arms and said I been bit on the ankle. His grandpa lifted his ankle up and there were two large fang marks on his left leg just above the ankle. His grandpa jerked the boy up and ran toward the chicken house. He ran through the gate with out ever unlocking it, and grabbed up the first chicken he saw and then he pulled his clasp knife out and split that chicken right down the middle, lifting the boys leg he slapped the split part of the chicken down on the two fang marks and held it there. In the mean time grandma had herd the yellowing and here she come on the run It almost made to boy want to laugh to see his grandma run, she was short, and big around as a wash tub, but when she wanted to move, she could pick-em-up and put-em-down. She came charging into the chicken yard and took the whole scene in at a glance. She reached into the pocket of her apron and pulled out a plug of good-money twist tobacco and popped it into her mouth and started chewing The boy was to say latter that with his grandpa holding him down and smearing a cut chicken on his leg, and his grandma chomping on the twist that it was the most exciting thing that had ever happened to him, if only his leg hadn't hurt so bad.

The chicken had turned a funny looking green when his grandpa took it of his leg, and let up on him, but then it was his grandma's turn to do her thing. Taking the chaw out of her mouth she slapped it down on the snake bite and took out a roll of twine she always carried around with her, and tied the chaw in place, then his grandpa picked him up and carried him back to the house and set him in the shade.

His grandpa said the chicken had pulled most of the poison out of the bite, but that he might still get sick, even with the chaw polities on it, so he would have to be watched for a day or so.

Along about sundown the boys head began to hurt, and the left felt like a cow had stepped on it, but all in all he was alive, and maybe now that trouble had taken another whack at him it would go along and bother someone else.

It was about midnight when the fever got so bad that the boy went out of his head and started yellowing, and fighting, and trying to get up and run away, His grandma held him down till his grandpa was able to fill a wash tub with water, then the two of them held him in it till the water was almost as hot as he was, but it did seem to do the trick. About four in the morning the boy calmed down and rested the rest of the dead, his grandma was to say latter, and the two grandparents were able to rest, or at least the grandpa did, grandma never left his side. The sun was coming up when the boy started to return to the world of the living. His eyes were still closed and he was just about to open them when he heard some one talking low and soft. He listened a moment, and realized it was his grandma, and she was praying. She said" Dear Lord, I know I ain't always done right, and maybe you don't cotton to all I say, but please lift this snake bite curse from my boy. I don't know what I would do if I was to loose him, he is the light of our lives, and makes living worth while to us. All our kids have grown and left us, and all we have left is this grandson to keep us young, and alive. We love him so, that if you was to take him, I do declare you might as well take the whole tribe with him, cause living would have no more meaning then a fish out of water."

They boy reached over and took his grandma hand in his and said here now grandma, I ain't going know where, I plan to stay with you forever. " Grandma said " forever is a long time son, lets just get through this and put it behind us, how ever I do wish you would be more careful when your out gal-a-venting around. That Duran snake could have killed you, and not only that you cost me one of my frying hen, not to mention a whole plug of twist." She then bent and kissed his head and went on to her bed, she was worn out.

The boy was to forever wonder which she was most upset about, the chicken, or the twist.

It was a few days latter and the boys strength was coming back when his grandpa came in with a tow sack in his hand. " Well now he said.... U got me a critter in here that you know real well". "What" asked the boy with suspicion in his eyes," well it's that ankle biting snake I reckon. Want to see it?." Nope...I done seen the business end of it once, and it was hanging off my leg then, I recon I've seen all the snakes I want to see this summer, besides how do you know it is the same one any way?." "Cause I went back where you got bit, and looked around for it. Found it coiled up under some buck brush. He tried to get me but missed, and my shotgun didn't. I don't think he'll biting any more people for a long time." "Sounds fine to me. I didn't like the business end of him the first time, so I don't cotton to much meeting him again, ether under the buck brush, or in your tow sack."

Grandpa left, and took his prize with him, and the boy set back in wonder at all that had gone on. First he killed a snake cause it had a killed one of his friend's. And now his grandpa had killed a snake cause it had bit him. Well.... he thought, there has to be a lesson here some where, but blamed if I can find it, but may be it ain't know lesson at all , only just more trouble, and that I can believe.

However it was noticed by others that in the future the boy fought shy of snakes. For in the past he would walk a mile to kill one, now he would walk a mile to avoid one, but maybe like he was to say later, snakes got there own ways of getting even, cause if you kill one, sooner or latter, its kin are going to come looking for you, and you never knew when they were going to show up and that was trouble he could do with out

5

August was over and September was coming in with full bloom. The heat was over, and they had four days of rain that the boy said would of sunk Noah's ark if it was still around. They spent time getting the cows unstuck from the mud that they had formed around the edge or the pond, and even when they pulled the jar-heads out, they would turn around and go right back. The boy said they ought just shoot the ones that kept doing this, but his grandpa said they were just like people. when the boys asked in what way, his grandpa said "well now....you can teach some folks a thing and they will learn it the first time, just like some of the cows learned that if they get to close to the water hole they will get stuck, but then you got that funny type of person that know matter how much you show them, they never learn, just like a few of these old heifers, they just keep going back and getting stuck, and will never learn. "Well" the boy said, " if that is the way it is, why don't we just get rid of the ones that never learn?" "Now son listen to me for a moment and I'll try to put this to you the only way I know how. Cows are like people in the respect that there are the get-in'ers and the bail-out'ers. There are some folks that just cant help getting into trouble, and as soon as they get out of one fix, there off and running and get into another. There the get-in'ers. Now the bail-out'ers are the ones always going around and getting the get-in'ers out of trouble. Neither one of the two types can help them selves. It's like if they tried to change, it would be unnatural, and would upset the whole works. Although I have heard of some that have changed, but mighty few, mighty few." " Couldn't we get rid of the get-in'ers and just keep the others ?" Well now... if we did that, the ones we would have left would all get together and draw straws some night and decide who would become the new get-in'ers, and we would have it to do it all over again. No well stick to the ones we already know and hope no more show up.

The boy knew there was a lesion in this, but sure couldn't see what it was. It was latter on in his life that he would remember this talk, and damn if his grandpa hadn't been right.

It was the next day when his grandpa told him that they had to go into town to get him enrolled into school. AHHH now grandpa, cant I stay here at home with you and grandma ? I don't cotton to much to school, and you know all I do is fight. Ever time one of these townies smart off and say something, I just up and pop them on the side of the head and the fight is on. Then I end up getting a licking, and then it just starts all over again. What I would like to know is why it's always us country folk who always get the butt kicking, and never one of the townies ?" "Well now...I cant answer that one, but maybe if you just closed off your ears and didn't listen and just go on about your business, and not be bopping heads, maybe you wouldn't get into trouble."

The boy thought about this for a few moments, and then said" All right. I'll keep my mouth shut, and my ears closed, and won't be hitting anyone. But what do I do if they hit me first ?" " Why then you just turn the other cheek." "TURN THE OTHER CHEEK ?. Are you sure that is what I am supposed to do "? I reckon, after all that is what it says to do in the good book." :well I'll give her a go, but what if it don't work, tell me now what am I supposed to do then ?" "Well now...I reckon then you'll have to bop some heads."

The boy got enrolled into the fourth grade, and everything seemed to go all right. Next his grandpa took him over to the five and dime and bought him two new pairs of Levi's, five pairs of socks, three shirts , and a new pair of shoes. The shoes was the only thing the boy didn't like. He always wondered why he just couldn't wear his moccasins. They were a Duran sight more conferrable, and a sight more warmer then the shoes. When he asked about it, he was told he had to learn to be civilized some time and it might as well start now as latter. To the boy's way of thinking if this was being civilized, then you could have it, shoes and all.

The first day of school the boy caught the school buss down at the mail box. As the buss pulled away he felt like that drowning man he had once heard about. He was sure he could see his life passing before his eyes. He took a slow look around the buss and looked at each person. They were all countries like him, so he felt a little better, not a townie among them. Maybe things were looking up after all. Maybe he was going to be going to a school this year full of countries. Maybe cows could fly too. The boy worked these thoughts over for awhile, and decided that maybe he would get it. He knew Duran well he was going to have to go to that Duran townie school and the thought of that just about turned his gut, At the next stop a little tow headed boy got on and looked around for a seat. All

the seats had one person in it already. Countries were
friendly to a point, but sitting lose together was pushing
things a bit far. The boy looked perplexed, and the buss
driver turned around and told him to sit down so he could
go on driving. Well this was something new. The bus cant
move until your sitting down, now this might be away to
keep the buss from ever reaching town, but even as that
thought crossed his mind, the buss driver got up out of
his seat and took the tow head by the hand and put him
in the seat next to the boy.

The two boys looked at each other, and the difference
between the two was like looking at daylight and dark.
The boy was Indian. He had jet black hair, a reddish color
to his skin. He was tall for his age. His eyes were jet black
and when he smiled his teeth were white and even. The
tow head on the other hand, was blonde, and real fair
skinned. He was shorter then the boy and had blue eyes.
He was missing one tooth from his uppers and two from
his lowers. The two boys looked at each other for a few
minutes, and then looked away. The boy had never seen
any one so white. He wanted to touch the tow head to
see if the white came off like white wash did, but then he
thought if he is white washed and I touch him it will wear
off and then he will have a mark and might get it trouble
with his family for marring up the paint job. No better not
touch him. The boy then scooted as far away from the tow
head as he could get.

The tow head felt like a goose with out feathers. He
looked around and saw that he was the only one on the
buss that was not dark, and this made him feel even worse,
then the boy next to him moved over and that just topped
it off. While this was going on the buss driver was having
jigger-fits with the buss.(Jigger fits is what a drunk goes
into when he is trying to sober up) the recent rains had

played hob with the road. The ruts were only half dry and ever now and then the buss would careen to the right or the left and try to take its cargo into the ditch. It was a most unaccommodating buss, and the driver was hard put to make it mind.

The antics of the buss was not troubling the children at all. As a matter of fact they were having the time of there lives. This was better then tire swings, or sliding down a grassy hill on a tow-sack, or even a trip to town. This was adventure in the highest. As the buss plowed from side to side, the children were swaying with it, and laughing all the while. Soon the swaying got so bad that the tow head slid in to the boys and the boy almost jumped out of his skin. He looked down at the tow head and just knew he would see dark stains on his white wash, but by zing's he was still white. "Say said the boy, don't that white stuff wash off?" Why how queer you do talk, no it don't wash off, it's just my color. What made you ask that for any way ?" " Well I just never seen anyone as white as you, for that matter I ain't never seen any one with white hair before either. What did your mom do to get you so white any how, stand in the light of the full moon with no clothes on cause ever one knows that would bleach anything out. "No, I don't think she did that, I think she ate some white paint, any way that is what she told me when I asked her about it one time." :well I reckon that would do it, but that sure seems like a lot of trouble to go to just make your kid white. I bet she had a gosh-awful belie ache after doing it?" "Well all I know about her ache was that she just said that I was a pain in the ass being born." :say now. You ain't no banker are you, there the only pain in the ass I ever heard of." NO I ain't no banker, but mom says I am a pain in the ass any way."

This was new hay. The boy had never heard of any one calling any one else a pain in the ass before except bankers. Maybe there were other kinds of ass pains he had never heard off. This was something he would have to take up with his grandpa.

The buss after a most adventuresome journey, and the buss drive swore latter that he had seen his life pass in front of him at least five times, but what bothered him was that it wasn't even interesting the first time much less then the fifth and vowed to make his life a lot fuller from then on, and eventually turned into the town drunk, finally arrived. The door opened up and the children got off. They looked around and stuck mostly with each other. They were standing in front of a two stories building. There were twelve rooms in the building for class rooms, then there was the janitor room, the offices, and four bathrooms. Two for girls and two for the boys.

The children herded them selves up the flight of steps and into the double doors and found them selves looking down a long hall. There was a desk in the middle of the hall with a fat woman behind it, who looked like on of the boys grandpas fattening hogs, and the boy swore latter when he saw her eating her lunch, that she made the same sound as the hogs with one respect, and that was his grandpas hogs had better manners, and didn't try to grab up ever morsel in sight, but at least saved some for latter. The porker, as the boy was to call her from then on, was counting heads, and taking names. First you went up to her desk and told her your name, then she pined a number on you. After that you went down the hall and looked for the number you had on you to match the number on a door. That is how you found the class you were going to be going into.

The boy found the number four and compared it with the number pined to his chest, and went in. The room was big and airy, with desks setting in neat lines about eight across and ten deep. He chose one over next to the window at the back and parked it. He was sitting there looking out the window when someone set down next to him, he turned and there set a pretty little girl. She had dark hair that hung to her shoulders, and gray green eyes. She wore a red ribbon in her hair, and she was smiling at him. The boy smiled back and was going to say something when a fat kid walked up to him and said your sitting in my seat. The boy looked up at him and said, " Say now, I don't see no name on this seat but mine. I set here first, and here I stay." OK for you. I'll be waiting on the play ground for you, cause your sitting next to my girlfriend and I mean to have your hide at noon." with that he turned around and walked off. The boy was mad, and at the same time a little scared, then the girl reached over and touched his arm and said, "he not my boy friend. He wants to be and won't let me alone, but he is not my boy friend." About that time the teacher walked in and class started.

The first day of school the teacher had all the kids stand up and give there names, and tell a little bit about what happened to them over the summer. The boy told about being bitten by a rattler, and the fat kid said Rocks, and this resolved the boy to thrash him even more at lunch. But by and by the teacher got them settled down and into there reading, and writing, and there numbers, and the morning past with out further miss-hap.

The lunch bell rang and the boy took out his fifty cent piece his grandpa had given him and set out for the drug store. That is where everyone went to eat if you didn't bring your lunch. He was just starting off the school ground when someone grabbed him by his left shoulder and spun him around. There stood the fat kid, and he was not alone. He had two boys with him. He said " Well now I am going to give you what for." Now the boy had been taught by his uncles that there is a time to talk and a time to fight. Seemed to him that the talking had already been said in the class room, so with out further a due, he belted the fat kid in the nose. Blood went everywhere, and the fat kid grabbed his nose and let out a howl that reminded the boy of one his grandpa coon dogs with a cold. When the fat kid grabbed his nose, the boy hit him in the gut, the boy was to say latter it was like hitting a bag o mush. This knocked the wind out of his adversary, and then the boy tripped the kid to the ground. The boy waited a minute to see if the kid would get up, and then turned around to walk off, that is when the fat kid's two friends jumped on his back. The boy went down under there weight and was trying to turn over when he heard someone say, " Hey now that ain't fair and then it was just plain ol'ned for the space of about five minutes. When the boy finally was able to look around who does he see but tow head. " Well now... said the boy, what got you into this fight. ?" " Well you see you're the only friend I got here and besides two on one ain't fair. " He turned his thoughts back to the boys they had been fighting and they were all laying on the ground holding there bellies and there noises. " I reckon our fight is over with these two for now, lets go eat."

After lunch was over and class had taken up again, the boy and the tow head was called to the office When they arrived at the door the boy turned to the tow head and said " Well if this goes like it always does, we'll catch ol'ned and the other's will go free." Don't seem fair to me." " Na, it don't work that way, were countries, and there townies, so countries always get the tar knocked out them, and the townies go free."

The two boys opened the door, and walked in. The porker had now taken up a station behind a long counter and was eating a candy bar. The boy walked up to her and said that they had been called to the office for sentencing, and wanted to know where they were to go. The porker leaned over the counter and said " So your the one that hurt my little Horace? Well I lay you will get your dues now." She turned and opened a door behind her and to her left, and said those two ruffians are to see you now." She then turned and motioned the two boys into the room.

Behind the desk set a man that the boy had never seen before. He was a young man maybe in his late 20's or early 30's. He had dark straight hair, and was dark of skin. He had brown eyes that had laugh lines at the corners. He had a smile on his face that showed his teeth to be white and even. When he stood up he was tall-6 feet or more, and he was dressed in a white shirt with a blue tie. His pants were dark blue and he had a narrow belt with two silver buckles holding them up. "Well, well, well. What do we have here now, two outlaws? I don't think so. You look like normal boys to me, but I've been hearing that you two were devils on the loose. Want to tell me about it"? First he looked at the boy, then at the tow head, then back at the boy. The boy shuffled his feet and then looked the man in the eye. His grandpa always said to look folks in the eye when doing business, cause if you could meet there eyes, and they could meet your eyes, then honesty would take over, and a good bargain could be struck. So the boy looked him in the eye, or better yet looked up at his eye's and said " Well I had a fight with this fat- at that moment the man held up his hand to stop the boy from talking and came from behind his desk and went over and shut the door. He said " The whole world doesn't need to know what they were discussing in here. Lets keep this private, shall we?."

The boy was liking this better and better. Always before when ever he got the boom lowered on his head the door was left open, and the whole world could here everything that went on. The man went back to his desk and set down. Now what was it you were saying before I stopped you? Please go on?" The boy said "Well like I said before, I had a fight with this fat kid." " Did you start it?" This was something new, never before had the boy ever been asked how the fight got started, He was just asked if he had been fighting, and when he said yes he go the belt. " No I didn't. I was going down to the drug store to get my lunch when this fat kid jumped me. He had two friends with him, but I did throw the first punch. Got him right on the nose, then I hit him in the gut, and tripped him to the ground. I started to go then and then his two friends jumped me when my back was turned." " Oh I know all about the fight, I set here in my office and watched it. What I want to know is how it got started? " "Well...., I guess it got started in the class room. I came in and set down in a desk, and then this girl came in and set down next to me. I looked at her and she looked at me . Then this fat kid came in and said I was sitting in his chair, and I told him it didn't have his name on it and I wasn't moving. He then said I was sitting next to his girl friend and that I had to move. I said I wasn't moving. He then said he would fix me on the school ground." Are you the boy that got bit by the rattler over the summer? " " Sure am. Here I'll show you the fang marks." With that the boy pulled up his pant leg and smooched down his socks and showed the man his marks. They had turned purple, and his grandpa said that after a time they would fade out to just two black dots. The man bent over and inspected the leg and shook his head. " Well your the first person I've ever met that had been bitten by a snake. Were you very sick after it happened ? " " Oh yes, but I got better after having a chicken and then a twist chew put on it. I did go out of my head for awhile, but grandma dunked me in a tub of water and that took care of that." The man shook his head and said well, well, then he said " Now lets get back to the fight. What do you think I should do to you?" "If it goes like it always has before, just belt me, and then I'll go back class." "Belt you, you say. Is that the way works ? " " Always has in the past, so I reckon it will be the same way now." The man turned to the tow head and asked him what his reason for getting into the fight was, and the tow head said it just didn't look to be a fair fight and that if it had just stayed with the fat kid and the boy he wouldn't have got involved, but was happy that it did happen cause he liked to fight, and that was a good excuse as any.

The man sent the boys out to set in the outer office, but the door was closed and they couldn't be sure. Soon the fat kid and his two friends came in and went into the office with the man, and they were in there a pizzen long time, then the two boys were called back in to the office to stand with the other three. The man laid down the law, and said there would be no more fighting, and that if there was all parties would be punished, and when the boy asked townies to, was told that any one caught fighting during school hours would get belting, and there would be no difference between townies and countries. They were then sent back to there class.

After school let out and the boy was getting on the buss to go home, when he saw the little girl that had been sitting next to him get into a car, then to his surprise the man came out and got into the car with her and drove away. The boy was to find out latter that the little girl was the man's daughter, and much latter that this same little lady would one day be his wife, how ever that is another story, and we won't talk about it now.

6

The ride home was uneventful except the buss kept trying to go into the ditch even though the roads had been dried out considerable. The boy and the tow head said latter that the buss driver smelled like he had been hitting the 40-rod, and in truth he had. The buss driver was just trying to live up to his vow.

When the boy got home, he went in and changed his clothes, and then went and did his chores. When he had finished them he cornered his grandpa down at the milk barn and told him about the talk he had with the tow head and asked just how many kinds of ass pain there was. His grandpa told him that when he got older they would have a talk, but till then not to worry about it but the boy kept up with the questions till his grandpa sent him to see his grandma and she thumped him on the head with her thimble, and told him to mind his own business if he had any and not to pester her with things he was to young to know about. This put all kind of ideas in his head, and he worked it over till supper was called, and then put it to rest for awhile.

That night as he was laying in bed he could here his grandparent talking, and they were talking about him, so he put his ear into over time and sucked up the talk like a sponge. He had a hard time following the talk, cause it seemed they were talking about how babies were born, and how his grandpa was hard put to answer his questions that day, and his grandma said if all they could teach at that school was such clap-trap as that, that the boy might as well stay at home and not be exposed to such business, but his grandpa said that wouldn't do and that the boy would find out about it some time, and his grandma said when sometime came, that that would be soon enough. Along about there the boy fell asleep, but in the days and even years to follow he would remember back to that talk and smile. Hell he already knew about how babies were born. All you had to do was watch a cow in heat and then let a bull get with in a country mile of it and the fun was on. The thing that the boy couldn't figure out was how people were suppose to do it. But if that was all the fuss that his grandparents were talking about, he figured that sooner or latter he would get the answer with out having to worry them with it, and so by and by he went to sleep.

The buss arrived at its usual time, and the boy got on to go to school. When his friend tow head got on they set together, and this was to be the routine for the next few years of there life during school. The boy told the tow head what he had learned about ass pain and the tow head said it made sense to him, cause having a kid could give a body a pain there, and from then on the boys looked at women in wonder, and awe to think that they did the same thing with them that the cow did with a calf, and they both agreed that it would be a pain in the ass to do something like that and that any one who would do a thing like that must be crazy or just liked pain.

They talked the thing over till they got to school and then other things came along that took there mind off of the matter of sex, but before it was forgot all together, the boys had decided to let it be, cause it could be of no use to them and it was best to let it alone and not be bothering with something that caused ass pain any way.

When they got into there class room the boy made a rude discovery. The fat kid had taken his place beside the girl. Well this just wouldn't do. He walked over and said "Your sitting in my seat." The fat kid said " Well what are you going to do about it" and a grin spread across his fat face. "Either you move, or I'll bust your nose like I did yesterday." " In the class room?" the fat kid asked." It don't matter much to me any way, the boy said, in here or out side, cause after I whip you then you will get belted by the man we saw yesterday." So will you". The fat kid blurted." Maybe so, but know matter how you look at it, I will only get one belting, you'll get two. One from me and one from him." This put the matter in a different light. The fat kid moved.

At lunch that day the boy took his sack lunch and went outside to sit on the steps with the other kids to eat. It was only on the first day of school that he got to eat in town, after that it was the bag as he called it. He was just sitting down when the tow head walked up and set down with him." What you got to eat to day" He asked. " Oh nothing much, just a sandwich, two plums and a fruit jar of milk. How about you?" " I got about the same only ma put in some onions. She says they keep down colds and might keep me from getting sick. About all they do that I can think of is give you bad breath.:"

About that time the fat kid came up." Well look at the hicks. Eating out side don't they let you eat inside at home." Now the boy was ready for him. "Nope you see there are

only two kinds of critters that eat inside. One is a grain
fed prize bull. The other is hogs. You don't look like a bull
to me, but you sure do look like a prize fattening hog. Say
now can you sound like one, cause from your looks you
must eat like one?" The fat kid started to hit at the boy
but caught him self in mid swing, for there standing about
them was the man. He looked down at the boys and took
out his lunch sack and said " Mind if I join you?" "It's such
a pretty day that I couldn't bear to sit inside a minute
longer." With that he set down hand opened his sack and
pulled out a sandwich and started to eat. The fat kid took
off to town feeling he had escaped with his life, and the
boy watched him go with a smile on his face.

Lunch hour passed with the boy and the tow head and
the man all talking about the weather, and what not. The
boy was to learn that when you got nothing else to talk
about, that talking about the weather is the easiest way
to pass time in a conversation. In his future he would have
many conversations about the weather, and it never failed
to pan out, that even with people he didn't know, or had
just met, that talking about the weather was a good way
to pass the time.

The fat kid left him alone for the remainder of the
week, and there were no disputes over the seating
arrangements. Eventually the children settled down to
getting there studies, and a kind of peace settle over the
class room.

History was the boys best topic, till the teacher told
them that the word history meant, when broke down
HIS-STORY. The teacher went on to say that history was
important because it showed you where mistakes had
been made in the past, and by looking at the past then
you would not make the same ones in the future. The boy
would have had to agree, except that it seemed to him

that ever country he studied about the folks there kept making the same mistakes the other countries had made, so nothing was ever learned, so that he lowed that he wouldn't waste his time with it, if all the people in those countries were going to keep making the same mistakes, and creating problems for ever body else and then, what good was the lesson any way. To his way of thinking, as soon as one king or queen got done creating troubles for ever one and then died off, along came another and did the same thing. Seemed like a circle to him, and ever one in those stories kept making the same mistakes over and over and know one seemed to notice it. So history was just a bunch of trials and problems, and headache's that could best be handled by leaving it alone, and not bothering with it, cause if you kept at a thing long enough, you were bound to start doing the same thing your self, and he had enough on his plate as it was.

When he tried to tell his teacher how he felt she told him not to worry about it, but to go along and learn it any way, that some day it would all make since, and he would remember she had told him so. He said he would try, but that the whole thing was above his head, and he still couldn't find any use for it.

When he got home and told his grandpa about it, his grandpa listened and then said that the teacher was right, and that the boy was right too. The boy said he had a headache and went down to the orchard, and stayed there till supper time. He never brought up the subject about history again. Like he said latter, with all those rights, some one had to be wrong, and wasn't about to try to figure that one out.

7

September came to close and ever one had settled into a routine that was to last them all till winter came to an end sometime in late April or May. It was now the third week of October and the family had just finished a week of tent meetings. Tent meetings were what they called the traveling preachers that came through in early fall and again in the spring. This meeting had to do with the evils of the season. The evils the preacher kept harping on was Halloween. He called it the devils holiday, and said that anyone that took it up was going to hell, and so on and so forth. He put such a fear into the little kids that ever time they saw a woman in a dark dress they thought they were looking at a which, and grandma said he sure shot her winter clothes to hell and back, as all she ever wore in the winter was a dark blue or black dress made of wool. She said ever time she went in the town from now on that the townies would think she was a which, and that she might put a hex on one of them.

She mulled this over for a time, and decided it might work for her. The next time she went to town she tried to convince the man that owned the hardware and feed store that if he didn't give her a good price that she might put a hex on him cause ever one said she was a which. He told

50

her that if she had come into his store on a broom and not showed up in a beat up old wagon that he might believe her, and until she did show up on a broom she would have to pay his prices, and in the mean time she could hex all she wanted to,, so long as she paid her bill. Grandma got mad and said she would take her business else where, and then the store owner asked her where she would go, she said down the road to the next town, and he said he owned the store there to. She got real hot then and told him he was a low life, and couldn't be trusted, he said he didn't care what she thought of him , but to just pay the bill and for her to run along and hex someone else. She paid the bill, and swore not to listen to anymore tent preachers who talked about Halloween.

The boy and his friend the tow head in the mean time had got together to decide what they would do for fun on Halloween. They kicked around a few ideas but the one they liked the best was dumping over out houses. They decided to wait till it got good and dark and then set out on there quest.

It was just past nine the night of Halloween and when the two boys met at the orchard. They shook hands and made a vow not to ever tell anyone about what they were going to do, and then spit in a circle that the boy drew on the ground, and that bound there lips for ever.

The first place they went was down the road to the Busshiehead's. They had two holler out house. Mr. Busshiehead said the reason for the two was that sometimes the family took the trots and when you had them you didn't have time to wait till the person was in the outhouse to get through, so he had built a double holler and said if more then two came down with the trots, they would have to hit the bushes.

The two boys got around behind and started to rocking the structure. It took them awhile, but by and by they got it over on its back. Next they went over to Manyhourses. There's was just a one holler so it went over real easy. The two boys kept it up till they had dumped over six all together. They were just starting in on there seventh one when they heard a noise inside the out house. Damn the voice said, that wind came up awful fast. I better get through and get to the house. The two boys looked at each other and grinned. They put there backs into it and gave a real big shove. There was a scream and a whole lot of thrashing around, and a lot of cussing. The two boys turned and there feet didn't hardly touch the ground till they were a mile away. When they came to a stop, they fell to the ground laughing and rolling around. "Now I don't know but I bet it sure was a surprise to who ever it was'. the tow head came back. " Well...we better get home for now" the boy said, and hope no one connects this with us. The two said good night and went there separate ways.

When the boy walked into the house his grandma said " Where in thunder have you been?" " I been out with tow" said the boy." Now you two hellions ain't been up to anything wrong have you, cause if you have I lay I'll take a switch to your back sides." " Na grandma, we ain't been doing anything wrong." The boy had his finger crossed when he said it, but what he didn't know was his grandpa was behind him, and when he turned around he saw his grandpa grinning at him. The boy got red in the face and went to bed as soon as possible.

The next day at school he saw the woman he called porker. She had a bandage on her head and looked real put out. It was latter that afternoon when he found out what had happened to her. Seemed she had went out to the country the night before to visit a friend of hers, and while she was there she had to go to the toilet. While she was in the out house, some no good had come along and tipped it over and she was caught in there for the longest time, and got a knot on her head, not to mention she was in the middle of peeing and when the house went over she missed the hole and ended up wetting on her self. It was also said that if she ever found out who done it she was going to press charges. The boy and the tow head got together and decided the only charges she could come up with would be violation of consutional rights. The boy said he had read the contusion in his history book and it didn't say anything in there about outhouses, so he guessed she couldn't do a whole lot even if she did find out.

At supper that night the boy's grandparents could do nothing but talk about all the trouble that had gone on the night before, and his grandma said it beat all how much meanness there was in the world. She also said if she was in the out house and someone came along and dumped it while she was in it she wouldn't rest till she had the culprit but the hair of the head. The boy got so uneasy that he for got to eat and left the table early, which caused concern with his grandma, who was one of those cooks that if you didn't eat up everything in sight when you set down to eat then you must be sick. She sought the boy out and gave him a good dose of salts, which as it tuned out kept him in the out house most of the night with the trots.

While he was sitting in the out house he got to musing about the last day or so. He decided that he wouldn't tip over any more of them, cause now he was having to send a powerful lot of time in one, so he guessed he was being paid back for being so mean. The only bright spot of all this and the thought that kept him smiling even though he was cramped up worse then if he had been eating green apples, was the fact that the porker had gotten hers, he only wished it had been her son, the fat kid.

8

The boy spent the night of October 31 sitting in the out house, and to here him tell it latter, you could discover a lot about a out house that you didn't know existed till you spent an ice age or so in it. When his grandpa asked him what he learned, he said that he never knew there could be so many different smells all wrapped up together in one place, and that it would just make your nose work overtime trying to sort them all out, and he figured that his nose had worked enough the last day or so to take a vacation, and that he would never look at one again with out remembering this last experience. His grandpa only said that it was punishment enough. The boy didn't ask him why he said that, but he had a fair idea.

November blew in cold and wet. The rain that had let up back at the end of September started all over again with a vengeance, and a renewed strength to turn the whole world into a mud hole.

When the boy wasn't helping pull stuck cows out of the mud, he was in school. A week before thanksgiving the boy was talking to the tow head (who he had taken to calling whitie) about how they were going to get a turkey for the holiday. Whitie said all they had to do was track one down and shoot it. The boy asked who in there right minds would let them ever have a gun. Whitie said he had a point, then the idea struck them that maybe they could trap one. They talked it over one afternoon coming home from school and decided to meet the next day which was Saturday, and see what they could come up with.

They met in the orchard about ten on Saturday and started to lay out there ground work for the great catch. The boy said there were turkeys that lived down in the bottoms about two miles from the house, and whitie said he had never heard of them. The boy said there were scads of them just hopping all over the place, and that catching them would be easy. whitie asked how they would go about it, and the boy said they would make a wire trap, and the boy told him you just took a hunk of wire about four feet long and made a loop in one end and made it fast to the ground by tying it to a peg. Then you took the loop and fixed it so that it was upright in the turkey run. When the turkey walked through it, the loop would catch around the body, and as the turkey tried to go forward it would tighten up and your bird would be caught. Whitie wanted to know if the boy had ever done it be for, and the boy said no, but he had seen his grandpa do it, so he reckoned he could to.

The two boys went down to the hay barn and got about twenty feet of bailing wire, and some wire cutters. Then they set off for the bottoms. The bottoms as the boy called it, was a deep valley where a old river bed cut through the center of the valley. There were oak, blackjack, hickory, walnut, pecan, and scrub brush in abundance. There were deer, turkey, rabbits, coon, muskrat, squirrel all over the place. It was hard to tell just where to set the traps, but the boys found some nuts on the ground and cracked them open and sprinkled them around the traps. Feeling that they had done all that they could do, they set off for home. If they only knew the trouble that the traps were to cause they would have taken them down, and swore off eating any kind of meat for ever, and give up on ever hunting or trapping again, but they didn't, and when your young its ok to make mistakes, just so you learn from them and not end up in the history books.

While the boys were setting traps for turkeys, his grandma was having turkey troubles of her own. It seemed that ol'man Highcorn had a turkey that was a wonder. He liked to wonder to the boy's grandma's hen house and eat up the chickenfeed, and while he was doing this he just naturally whipped all the chickens in sight. This had become a problem, and his grandma had talked with Highcorn about it in the past, but finally the bird had got cross-grained of her when it broke one of her prize hens neck. When she found the chicken laying on the ground, and the tracks of the murdering turkey all around it she blew her top. This was more then a body could stand, and if that Duran Highcorn couldn't keep his bird at home, and do right by his neighbors, then she would lay for the culprit and fix his wagon when nxet he chose to visit her hen house with out an invention.

She went to the back of the well house where his grandpa kept his rolls of wire fencing. She shoved a roll o chicken wire over and unrolled about twenty feet of it. She then cut it off and standing the wire back up set out for then hen house. When she got there she put the wire across the top of the hen yard fence, she hooked it down all around the edges, and made it tight. Then she took her cutters and cut the wire in half. She reasoned that when the turkey showed up and tried to fly over the fence like he did in the past that he would land on the wire room of the pen. He would get to walking around and come to the weak spot, and when he did he would fall through and be trapped inside the yard. She got the idea from a book she had been reading about castles in England, and how they had secret panels and trap doors and such. She had been in a sweat to see if they worked, so now she had her chance..

She completed her task and went back to the house to wait and see what would happen. She got to working and forgot about the trap for the moment. It was at noon when grandpa came in and said, " Well I see high corn's bird is back for another visit." "What I lay I got him this time." and grabbed up her old shawl and out the door she went. Now women do beat all I ever heard tell of his grandpa thought, but went along behind her to see what was up.

The bird had come over for another free meal and when he flew over the fence he landed on the wire roof. He walked about for a while and finely hit the weak spot and fell through just like she had planned. She was so proud of her self she was beaming, when she got to the yard she found the bird eating up everything in sight, and causing all manner of ruckus with her chickens. She opened the door to the pen and went in. What happened next his grandpa was to say latter just took the wind out of him. Grandma advance upon the bird with the thought in mind of thrashing it with in an inch of its life then taking it back to Highcorn and telling him to keep his critters at home or next time it would end up in her pot. The turkey had other ideas. He raised his head and started to jump and hop around the pen. When grandma got close enough, the bird took a beak full of hide and hair out her. Grandma looked at her arm and saw the blood coming out of the wound and she, to here grandpa tell it, went in stone cold nuts. She grabbed the bird by the neck with her left hand and punched it in the head with her right. The bird threw his legs up and caught hold of the front of her dress with its feet and latched on to. Next it started to flail its wings in grandma's face, and this got her mixed up and she fell to the ground still holding the bird by the neck. By this time there was just plain old Ned breaking loose in the hen yard. The chickens were all hoping, and running and jumping around and squawking and flapping there wings cutting up to beat the band. Grandpa said latter that the whole thing reminded him of what a chinese fire drill would be like if he ever saw one. Grandma in the mean time had had about enough. She and the turkey were rolling around on the ground and the turkey was fighting for all he was worth, only thing is he had never met a critter like grandma. She got both of her hands around the neck and started to choke the bird. She held on for dear life till it was just a pile of feathers laying on the ground. Grandma kept her grip for about five or six minutes more then let go. She got up off the ground and then bent over and picked up the bird by the neck. "Well pa I reckon we got our turkey dinner, and all the trimmings." "Yep was all grandpa said. He didn't want to bring up the fact that it wasn't there turkey, not after watching her wring that bird's neck. In the mood she was in if she got mad at him, she might decide that a double killing just might make her day, and besides, his neck wasn't much bigger then the one she had just been doing battle with. Nope, better to say nothing, and just go along with it. He would deal with Highcorn latter if he had to.

While all of this was going on, the boys were walking back to the house, and when they heard about the fight they were put out that they had missed it. the boy said he would have give anything to of seen grandma scraping with a turkey, and that it was most likely the funniest thing that had happened in a long time. How ever it was noted that he said this to grandpa latter down at the milk house, and not in front of grandma. They both got a good laugh when grandpa told about it, and they laughed till they cried. When it was talked about in front of grandma though , it was always done with sober faces, and spoken of in awe. If they had spoken of it any other way, there would most likely been three wrung necks instead of just one.

The next day the two boys went back to the bottoms to see how there traps panned out. The first two were empty, but in the third they had got a skunk. The critter wasn't happy at all. It had to spend the night with its head in a noose that cut into its neck when ever it moved so it was good and mad by the time the boys had showed up. They could smell it before they ever got to it The boys came as close as they could from down wind. And looked into the clearing where there captive was lodged. They looked the situation over for a moment or two then backed off a ways to talk the thing over. Whitie was for just jumping on the thing and holding it down and getting the noose off and then turning it loose. They boy said to go ahead if he wanted to, but to give him a running start first, cause sure as water is wet, someone was going to stink to high heaven and he didn't want it to be him. Whitie then thought up the idea of just starving the critter in to surrender, but the boy said that would take a pizzen long time, and even if it did work they would have to fatten it back up to turn it loose, and he had already had a bout with feeding robins, and what they ate was bad enough, and he just couldn't began to think up all that a skunk would eat, and didn't want to find out.

The boy finely hit on the idea of holding the skunk down with a long stick that was forked at one end, and while he held the thing down, then Whitie could get the noose off. Whitie said it ought to work and agreed to give it a go. The boys searched around till they found a limb from a blown down tree that was about ten feet long. It took them awhile to break the limb off and trim the suckers off and then whittle down the forks so that they would be short enough. The boy took the stick and he and whitie walked back to the clearing where the skunk was having a black and white fit.

They got as close as they could with out getting sprayed and the boy started to push the forked end toward the skunk. He got the forks over the back of the skunks back and eased them into place behind the skunks head and then pushed the forks into the ground holding the skunk immobile. Whitie eased himself up to the skunk and bent down and eased the wire from around the skunk's neck and off over his head. Once he had the wire off he turned around and ran back to the boy.

Once that Whitie was out of the way the boy let up on the stick and that is when ol'ned broke loose the skunk had had one whole day and night to get good and mad. In skunk talk he was a pissed off pole cat. When he felt the pressure let up from his neck, he cut loose. He turned toward the boys and made a run at them. The boys in the mean time was wasting no time in trying to put as much distance as they could between themselves and the skunk. They weren't fast enough . The skunk ran between them and then filled the air with a smell that while it is a love potion to the skunk is just down right repulsing to anyone else. He sprayed the boys with his home grown perfume, and didn't even charge extra for giving them a double dose.

The boys in the mean time were doing everything in there power to keep out of the skunks way with out much success. Whitie caught a good dose in the chest and face, while the boys was covered from butt to head. The two boys fell to coughing and spitting and there eyes were watering so bad they kept running into trees and each other, and finely fell to the ground and tried to rub the smell off on the dry grass. They had no luck. The skunk stood back and watched for a second or two then feeling that he had gotten even, turned and with his tail in the air made a dignified escape into the woods.

After about twenty minutes or so, the two boy's eyes quite spouting water and they were able to see where they were going. They got up off the ground and made a quick retreat toward home. There families were to say latter that they could smell the boys coming for a country mile and would of packed and moved if there had been time to of done it.

When the boys reached the orchard and parted ways, the last ting the boy heard whitie say was that if his mom had thought of him as being a pain in the ass in the past, the good lord only knew what she would think of him now, and he sure was hard put to have to here it. The boy had to agree although he had said nothing. When the boy reached home, he was met at the door by his grandpa who had a rag over his nose and mouth, His grandpa told him to go along to the milk barn and he would be down directly. The boy went off down to the barn and set down on a hay bail to wait his judgment.

His grandparents showed in a bout half an hour. His grandpa had a number ten wash tub and some soap. His grandma was packing some clothes and some vinegar. They made him strip off and then stand in the wash tub while his grandma poured the vinegar over his head and let it run down his body. After he was good and soaked his grandpa filled the tub up with water so now there was a water and vinegar mix and told the boy to scrub him self with the lye soap. The boy did as he was told and scrubbed him self till he swore that he would loose his hide and probably be bleached as white as Whitie. This thought shook him up so bad he almost cried, but crying would only add insult to injury and he figured that that wouldn't do. So he gritted his teeth and bowed his back and scrubbed and rinsed most three or four times. He finely got the smell out enough so that he didn't smell so ripe, but it would still be sometime before he was allowed to sleep with the windows closed, much less get to set for very long in a room with the rest of the tribe with out them making faces and poking fun him.

When the two boys met again Whitie said his mom now said he was not only a born pain in the ass, but smelled like one too. The boy said he knew what he meant, cause his folks kept asking which way the wind was blowing so they could make him stand in front of the window as the air blew out. The boy said he was getting powerful tired of standing in front of the window like that, but guess they knew what they were doing even though it made him feel like a banker at a working mans meeting. The boys did agree on one thing, and that was that skunks could be the most tiresome critters they had ever met, and vowed to have nothing else to do with them even if ever one of them starved to death.

The rest of November went with out mishap, and the thanksgiving dinner was a great success for grandma, even when she said that the meal was provided by a thief and murder, and laughed. Highcorn showed up in the after noon and asked if anyone had seen his turkey, and grandma said the only turkey on the place was the one that had been the guest of honor at the feast, and Highcorn said he reckoned that they were talking about two different birds, and grandma said that her bird was one that had been gotten after a power of fighting, and Highcorn said his bird didn't fight, and grandma, said not any more I reckon. So he left still looking for his bird and grandma and grandpa broke the wish bone and looked at each other in such a way that the boy was to for ever wonder about it.

For the record, the boys did catch a turkey, but the thing thrashed them so bad with its wings, and pecked them so that they had to let it go, and from then on the boys swore that they would be shot to flinders before they would have any more truck to do with traps and there like, cause all they were good for was getting a body into trouble and they both knew that trouble came to you on its own, and it didn't make a lick of since to go looking for it.

9

November passed on with out further a due, and December came in on soft gentle clouds and gentle breeze that some times happen in Oklahoma, but everyone knew that it would change, and sure enough it did. Half way through the second week dark clouds rolled up out of the north and the wind picked up and went to howling around the eve's of the house so bad that grandma said that the ghosts of Halloween that had been taking a day off had woke up and decided to exercise there voices. The boy had to agree, and spent a couple of nights waiting for one to appear, but when it didn't happen gave up on it and decided that it was just the wind, and to not bother with it and loose any more sleep over ill-mannered spooks that just wanted to make noise and not let you see them, so he went to sleep.

It was the second day of the wind kicking up a fuss that the snow came. At first it was just soft flakes dancing on the wind, but it soon turned into sleet-snow mix, and then wind seemed to go crazy. It bounced off the walls and rattled the windows so that grandpa swore that the cold maker was trying to get in the house to freeze them all. The cold maker became the boy's worst fear.

The cold maker was a story that the boys grandpa told on cold winter nights. It was an old story, and his grandpa would lite his old pipe, and sit down in his easy chair that had been in the family and was sacred to his grandpa cause it was made of buffalo horns and hide. It weighed a ton and was hard to move so his grandma said, so it had set in the same place in the house for the last twenty years, and took up a powerful lot of space. It was a grand old chair that had been made by the boy's great-grandpa on the trail of tears, so it was even more precious to the family because of that, and it was in this chair that his grandpa always set when ever he held court.

Once the pipe was lite, and grandpa had his butt in the chair just right, then the story would commence.

Grandpa would say "Well now.... the cold maker is not a man, or a beast. He is a spirit and one that if you got hold of it you would be hard put to let go of. The cold maker came from the north, and he lived in a ice cave up there and was in charge of the north wind, snow and ice. He didn't like anything that was warm, and that was why he sometimes froze trees till they split, and anything that had to do with the sun. He hated all warm blooded things, and was only happy when he was causing trouble and making a ruckus with them. It was on the trail of tears that the cold maker had out done himself on the people. When the army of the great white father moved the people from there southern homes to the Oklahoma Indian territory it was in the late fall, going into winter. The cold maker watched from his cave the goings-on of the people, and decided to make war on them. First he sent his scout, the snow owl, so that he could get a first hand account of all that was taking place.

After he had all the news he could rake up on the people and knew just what all was going on. He sent his sister, cold-slanting-rain, to make the trail muddy and hard to walk on. Then he sent his brother, he-who-makes-sick-in-winter, and had him bring his chills, and fever on the people. Next he sent his friend, life-taker, and had him take the old ones and the young. Cold maker was doing right well by him self by now, and watched with interest the amount of graves that were piling up. Once the old and the young had been removed, the cold maker made his self known. First he froze wet mud and made the walking hard, so that it cut the shoes of the people, next he brought his wind from the north to thrash the wagons, people, and even the trail its self. Soon fire wood was short, and then the cold maker brought his cousin in to the picture, his name was He-who-takes-the-game. Soon all the animals were gone and the people began to starve. The cold maker then sent his ice sprites to lace the trees with ice sickles so that when the people walked under them the sharp sickles would drop off and some of the people were injured and died. The cold maker was having a grand old time with the people, soon though he grew tired, and needed to sleep. While he slept the clouds moved out of the way and the sun could peak through. The God above looked down and saw the trouble that the cold maker had been making and he cried, and when his tears hit the earth they turned into crystal rock. One of the people found one and when he held it up the sun looked through it and the man noticed that when the sun looked through the rock, that heat came out the other side. The man got together some sticks and old leaves and held the rock so that the sun could look through it to the small pile of brush. Soon a think tendril of smoke came up and then a small flame appeared. The man took the rock away and blew gently on the small fire and low it grew. He called the people together and showed them what he had found and how it worked. The people started to be happy, for now they knew that the God above saw them and would help them. They got in a circle and told the God above that they needed help, for to have fire was good, but all the brush was wet and they needed a big fire to warm away the cold maker. The God above talked with the trees and told them the problem, and the trees were going to help. The people rejoiced and sang a song of prayer to the God above. Soon the people had a large fire going, and with more and more trees falling, they soon had a fire so big that its heat reached the cold maker. When he woke up he thought spring had come, so he called for his tribe and had them all got to sleep for he thought his time for making mischief was over for that time. Spring came to the call of the God above and helped the people to gain back there strength, and the people were able to go on to there new home that he white father said would be there as long as the wind blew, and the grass grew, and the water flowed. So the people came at last to the assigned lands and lived there to this day. They never forgot the cold maker or the crystal rock, or the trouble that they had on the trail of tears."

His grandpa got quiet, and listened to the wind as it beat against the side of the house and said " the cold maker is out there and is still mad at the way he was tricked by the God above, but he cant do anything about it, except try to get even from winter to winter. Now boy run along to bed, its late and we have things to do tomorrow." the boy told his grandparents good night and went off to bed. After he had gotten undressed and into bed, and was laying there under his quilts all snuggled down in the goose down mattress, he turned his head and looked out the window and what he saw there most scared three lives out of him, for there hanging right in front of his window was a sickle as big around as his wrist and about three feet long. He stared at it for the better part of five minutes, then he got up and went to the window and pulled the curtain. He reasoned that if he couldn't see the cold makers, ice fingers, then the cold maker couldn't see him...maybe. But by closing the curtain at least he wouldn't have to look at it and that helped some.

The wind blew and the snow and ice kept up there onslaught for the rest of the week and the boy and his grandparents went outside only when they had too, which was in the mornings to feed the chickens and the hogs, and to do the milking. But at the end of the week the cold maker let up, and the skies cleared in the afternoon. The boy told his grandma that he was going down to his orchard for awhile, and she said to go along and get out from under her feet, that looking at him and his grandpa for the last week all day long had about give her the fan-tans, and she needed some time to be by her self or else she was going to blow like a steam pot.

The boy dressed warm, and even put on a extra pair of socks. He made his way across the field to the trees and was thinking about the trees in the legend of the cold maker and all that they had done for the people, and how friendly they looked even covered up with ice and snow.

When he got there he walked among them for awhile and was glad he had so many silent friends, cause this was the way he thought of the trees in the orchard, as his friends. He was walking along when his foot came down on a slick spot and his feet flew up and when he fell he hit the back part of his head on a hard object under the snow. He closed his eyes and slipped into darkness he felt the icy finger of a snow flake on his cheek, and his last thought was cold maker.

The wind picked back up as a new front moved in, and grandpa was hard put to keep his balance coming back from the milk barn. When he got into the house grandma was in the kitchen getting supper on so he set down in his chair to read the sale ad that had come in the paper he had bought the last time he was in town. About three hours had slipped by when grandma leaned into the room and looked around. "Say now pa, have you seen chch.? He went out just past noon and I haven't seen him scence, and now its coming on to dark and I am getting worried." Nope, I ain't seen him. Where did he saw he was going off to .?" "Why where he always goes, to his orchard. You don't reckon he's still there do you. Seems like he should have been home long ago." well now...I'll give him about another fifteen minutes and if he ain't home by then I'll go fetch him."

Grandpa spoke like he wasn't worried, but grandma knew different, cause even as he was saying he would wait he was up and getting into his coat. He got his hat on and pulled it down tight, the pulled his gloves on and went to the door. If I ain't back by full dark put a lantern in the window so's I can see, cause if this turns into a blizzard I might be hard put to see where to go. She said ok and even as he went out the door was lighting one up and heading for the window that faced the orchard.

It took him awhile to reach the orchard, and only realized he was there when the limbs began to hit him in the face. He stopped and looked around. There were know tracks to follow because the snow had filled up the boys foot prints. He decided to search deep into the trees cause that was where the boy liked to play. He was walking along and calling out for the boy to answer when he saw something that seemed strange. There laying on its side was a cedar tree. Now where did that come from he wondered, and walked over to look at it. There were know cedar trees in this place, or none he had ever seen and he had lived here for ni-on to thirty years, so now how did this tree happen to be here.? He reached over took hold of the green flat foliage that passed for leaves and pulled. When he pulled the cedar it rolled to the right a few feet, and there under it lay the boy. His grandpa bent down and scooped him into his arms and held him close. He pulled the boys face close to see if he could feel his breath. He could just make out a small puff of air against his cheek. He turned and walking as fast as he could headed for the house, and even though he was not aware of it he was saying over and over again Please God, Please God.......

It was the light in the window that finely led him home, and he said latter if that lamp hadn't been in the window he and the boy would still be out there come spring. When he reached the house he was almost stiff from the cold and swore latter that if he would have had to of gone on much further, he and the boy would have been froze statues, and that so distressed him that he spent the rest of the winter as close to the fire as he could, and swore that he would take up the ways of bears, if he lived to see another winter, cause bears holed up and slept the winter through, and that beat this walking around in snow and ice all to flinders.

When he reached the door he kicked the bottom a couple of times and grandma opened the door. The heat from inside of the house felt so good grandpa almost passed out. Grandma reached out and took the boy from his arms and carried him into the kitchen where she had a fire going that was the granddaddy of them all. The old wood stove was Cherrie red and grandpa said latter that you could of lit a match off of it two feet away. She laid the boy on the kitchen table and then scooted the whole thing over close to the fire. She then started to undress him. As she worked she kept up a running conversation with grandpa. She asked where he had found the boy, and then wanted to know why it was so Duran long to get back home. When she heard about the tree laying on the boy and the kind it was she paused and looked at grandpa to see if he was joking, and when she saw he wasn't just shook her head and went back to work.

After taking all the boys clothes off she then started to wet him down with cool water. She would get him wet then let the heat from the stove dry him out, and she kept this up till color started to come back into the boy. It was about four hours after she started the treatment that the boy groaned and opened his eyes. The first words were cold maker. Grandma vowed cold maker indeed. I lay you will think cold maker, more like life taker.

As the boy woke up more and more, he started to hurt. At first it was just a little tingle, then it started to set in to burning till he thought he was on fire. His grandma said it was the hide thawing, and now the blood would start to move into the places it had been froze out of, and the boy howled that if this was more then a body could stand and to put him back into a snow drift cause it didn't hurt and pester ya till kingdom come. His grandma told him to shut his head up or she would thump him till the gentiles came home, and he said he didn't care what she did cause she couldn't make him feel worse then this and any thing might be an improvement over this torture. The boy said latter that if he had it to do over again he would have tried to of found a better spot to get hurt in, cause dieing ain't so bad, but coming back to life was just more trouble then it was worth, and he hope that if it ever happened to him again that folks would just go on and let him pass and not bullyrag him into making another appearance into life cause it wasn't worth all the pain and suffering it caused.

The pain lasted well into the night and it was about three in the morning that the pain let up enough for him to sleep . His sleep was that of the bone weary and wrung out. He slept right through breakfast and lunch and didn't wake up till seven the next evening. His grandma had kept up a quiet vigil over the boy. She watched his color, and took his temperature, and listened to his breathing, and said latter that the whole business had taken ten years off her life and she sure was put out about it cause she was growing old and didn't have that kind of time to waste on such foolishness as this, and hoped that the boy would remember this when he got older and realize that he was the cause of her not getting to live out a full life cause of all the worry he had caused her and how sad he would feel when she was gone and he was the big cause of it. This caused the boy to cry and he swore to repent of his evil ways and do good if it shot him to flinders, and she said for him to not bother about repenting, but to just stay out of trouble, and he said he dodged it ever chance he got, but that trouble just seemed to sneak up on him and grab him at the most fearsome times, and she told him that some people were like that and he must be one, so from now on he must watch out even more, and she said she and grandpa would help him and he said he would do his part, so near tragedy ended with grandma and the boy hugging each other and crying and then they parted on good terms, but grandpa had kept his mouth shut and stayed on the side lines till he saw how the wind was going to blow, and when he seen ma wasn't going to have a Egyptian fit, he came into the room and told the boy how lucky he was and that the cold maker was after him and that he must be good and watch out, and the boy said he didn't want to have any truck with the cold maker or any of his kin, and his grandpa said he didn't either , so they shook hands and vowed as how they would leave such things alone and not mess with them from then on, and then grandpa left and the boy went back to sleep.

The next morning after his grandpa came in and told him to get dressed that he needed some help in the milk house. The boy dressed and then they walked down to the milk house with out talking.

When they got to the milk house and went inside his grandpa pointed at a bail of hay and the two walked over and set down. His grandpa thought a moment and then asked the boy if there were any cedar trees in the orchard. The boy said no, and then asked why. His grandpa then told him about how he had found him laying under a cedar, and how that that was probably what saved his life. The boy asked how, and his grandpa said that when he found the boy with the tree on top of him that the tree was all covered with ice and snow and that if it hadn't been for the tree the stuff would of covered him and he would have froze to death. The boy said that he wanted to see the tree cause he was sure that there was no cedar trees in the orchard. He said that there were oak, black jack, some elm and a few post oak, but no cedar, and he knew ever tree down there on a first name bases. Grandpa said after milking and the chores were done they could walk down there and see.

They finished there chores in record time, and after telling grandma where they were going set off. The wind had died down some but was still kicking up puffs of snow now and then. The walked with there heads bent and there hands deep in there pockets, cause even with gloves on the air was such that it ni-froze any exposed skin. They had mufflers wrapped around there heads and there hats were pull down tight. When they reached the clearing where the boy had fallen there was the tree just like grandpa had said. They also made another discovery and that was that the tree had been cut down, and fresh cut at that. They could see ax marks and there was still some sap coming out. The two walked around the tree and looked at it, then at each other, and shook there heads. The boy vowed he had never seen this tree before, standing up or laying down and had no idea where it came from. His grandpa thought a minute then said the only thing he could think of was that part of the story of the cold maker and how the trees had come to the rescue of the people and that this might be like that, but the boy said that those trees had fell down and that this one had been cut so there was a difference, and his grandpa muttered true, that's true. They looked awhile longer and went on back to the house, and when they got there the boy said that maybe it was the God above that had done it, and that he didn't have time to ask the trees to do it for him, and even if they could have they were the wrong type of trees, and what was needed was a cedar, so the God above had cut down one some place else and brought it to the clearing and covered him with it. His grandpa lowed that that had to be it, cause nothing else made since, and he was tired of trying to figure it all out and that it was just a mystery to him and when something like this happened not to question it, but be grateful for it and give the God above praise, and not ever forget that it was him that done it.

They were both happy with this thought and decided to let it rest with that.

10

It was rocking along toward Christmas, and the family was running around and trying to keep secrets from each other. The boy knew what he wanted to get his grandparents, but he had to get into town to do it, and the only time he was in town was when he went to school, and that didn't hardly enough time to shop during lunch, and the buss driver wouldn't wait in the afternoon when school was out for him to walk down town so he was hard put to get his shopping done. His grandpa solved the problem on the last Saturday before Christmas when he ups and said he had to go to town and would the boy like to go along.?

They left after the morning chores were done and got into town about eleven or so. Grandpa told the boy to meet him back at the feed store by one. This was just new hay to the boy. He was going to have two hours to wonder around town, and that had never happened to him before, so reckoned that he was growing up some for his grandpa to trust him so.

He went to the five and dime store to see if the things he had been looking at were still there. Over the past year he had managed to save ten whole dollars and this was

what he was going to buy his Christmas with. He had
seen a leather belt with a real chrome buckle and some
fancy white stitching on it that he wanted to get for his
grandpa, and for his grandma there was a salt and pepper
shaker with a napkin holder he had seen her looking at
back in the summer. He hoped that they hadn't been sold
When he got to the store and went in the first person he
ran into was the girl that set next to him at school. The
girl smiled at him and said "HI". He smiled back and said
the same thing, then he asked her what she was doing
there and she said she had come in with her father and
that he was looking for a new hat because his old one was
falling apart and if there was a thing her dad couldn't
stand it was a cold head. The boy had to agree and said he
was there to shop for Christmas, and she asked him if she
could go along and watch and he said sure.

They went to the isle where the house ware were kept
and he found the shakers and the napkin holder, and the
girl said that they were just the fanciest things she had
ever seen and the boy said they were for his grandma,
and the girl said that his grandma would just swoon
over them, this made the boy proud, and happy, and he
said he couldn't wail till Christmas morning and see his
grandmas face and the girl said it would be worth a fifty
dollar's to see her face. Next he went to where the leather
goods were being shown and found the belt. He told her
he was buying this for his grandpa and she said that her
dad always said you could tell the kind of man you were
dealing with by the way he kept his pants up. That if he
had a good belt on that it meant that he was honest, but
if it was ragged or if he didn't have one on that meant he
was a low life because he didn't care if his pants stayed
up or not, and so you couldn't trust that person, and it
was better to wait till you found one that did take pride

in how there pants stayed up, because that person would worry about such a thing was responsible and would keep there word.

The boy took his goods up to the counter and got in line, and the girl went with him. She was talking a mile a minute and the boy was hard put to get a word in edge wise when he heard a familiar voice and felt a hand rest on his shoulder. He looked up into the eyes of the same man that he came to know as the principle of his school. The girl took his other hand and said daddy, I want you to meet my friend. Her dad said we already met, and then asked the boy how he was doing and the boy said he was tolerable, and that he was just doing his Christmas shopping, and then asked if he had found the hat he had been looking for, and he said no that he would have to look else where, but that he had found some ribbon his wife wanted him to get. He then looked at his daughter and said Leeann are you through with you shopping and she said yes, and that she had just been following the boy around while he shopped and had been keeping him company.

The person in front of the boy had gotten his business out of the way and the boy laid his goods on the counter and the clerk totaled it up It came to ten dollar's and fifty cents. The boy forked over the ten and said it was all he had, and the clerk said it wasn't enough. The boy asked if he could just pay the ten and owe the rest like they some times did at the feed store, and the clerk said that they didn't run accounts here, and that if he didn't have enough money he would just have to put something back, or find something cheaper, and the boy said that that wouldn't do, that he had his heart set on these gifts for his grandparents, and come judgment day he would have them. He then asked if he could work the fifty cents off by cleaning or hauling or what ever, and the clerk said they didn't do that either.

while the conversation was going on between the boy and the clerk, liana and her dad were hearing ever word of it. The man reached into his pocket and took out a fifty cent piece and eased it in to the boy's right rear pocket. Then he tapped the boy on the shoulder and asked him if maybe he didn't have any more money on him the boy said no, only ten dollar's and the man said well why don't you check your pocket's and see. The boy said it was a waste of time but did it any way. When he found the fifty cent's he looked at it like it was a miracle and was hard put to explain it, and the clerk looked at him like maybe he was trying go pull a fast one or something, but took the money just the same and wrapped up the boys goods and handed them to him The boy went outside and stopped and looked about. He then run his hand into ever pocket again to see if there was any more money he missed, but came up empty handed, and was more perplexed then ever, and was in a sweat to find out where that other money had come from.

He was standing on the walk outside the five and dime mulling this over when leeanna and her dad came out. Her dad said it was a good thing he had that extra money, and the boy said that was just it he didn't have any extra, only just one ten, and he was stumped if he could explain it. The man told him to just except it as a fortuneious find and not to worry about it. The boy said he didn't know anything about fortuneious , but was hard put to explain where that fifty cents came from and that it sure was a mystery to him. The man just laughed and he and his daughter walked off down the street.

The boy walked around town and then went on back to the feed store to meet his grandpa. He had his bundle of gifts in a brown sack and was feeling real grown up. When he got to the feed store the owner Mr. Thompson asked him what was in the sack, and they boy told him it was Christmas gifts for his grandparents, and they were the gaudiest things ever, and Thompson said he would like to see them so the boy opened the sack and gave him a peak. Mr. Thompson said they were real fine gifts and that he couldn't have done better if he had tried, and the boy felt proud and said he couldn't wait for Christmas morning, and he was most ready to bust. Mr. Thompson told him not to cause then there would be a big mess if he busted and then he would have to clean it up and that would just create more work for him and he already had more on his plate then he needed. The boy laughed and said he wouldn't.

By and by his grandpa showed up and went into talk with Mr. Thompson and then came out and told the boy to load up and then they set out for home. The boys grandpa eyes twinkled and he was laughing and smiling all over the place, and kept looking at the bag clutched in the boys hand, and ever now and then would ask if the boy had gotten his business taken care of, and the boy always said yes, and wouldn't say any more. Grandpa tried to coax out of the boy what was in the bag, but the boy was hard headed and wouldn't tell and grandpa got to fretting over it so much he almost drove the wagon into the ditch, and then he set up and kept his eyes on the road, but ever now and then he would glance at the bag and frown, and then he started in on the questions again, and the boy was hard put so's not to get trapped and tell, and began to know how the skunk felt being cornered and all and not able to get away and vowed that if he could he would spray his grandpa if he could to get him to let up on the thing. This went on all the way home.

When they got home the boy jumped down and ran up to his attic room leaving his grandpa to park the wagon an unhitch the team. In his room he closed the door and put the latch in place cause he didn't want any one to break in while he was wrapping the gifts. He took some old newspaper and some twine and with a lot of concentration and a few false starts got the thing done and over with. He then set back and studied his handy work and was prouder then ever.

After supper the boy went up to the attic and came down with his gifts, and showed them to his grandparents. They got in a sweat to hold them and he said they couldn't touch them till Christmas morning. His grandma said they had to have a tree if this was going to be a proper Christmas, so the boy and his grandpa went back to the orchard and got the tree that had saved the boys life and brought back to the house. When they had it standing up in the front room grandma said it looked naked with out and decorations on it, so the boy spent the next three nights making popcorn links and colored paper chains. He made so many that his grandpa said that the place was starting to look like a dungeon with all the chains hanging around and he didn't know if he would be able to sleep for fear of waking up and finding out he was chained to the bed. Grandma told him to hush and go see if he could find some silverweed to put on the tree, so he left vowing he might move to the barn till all this foolishness was over, but he said it with a smile, and the boy knew he was having as much fun as he was.

While grandpa was out on his errand grandma went to her sewing chest. She got out some gold thread and she and the boy cut it into lengths of ten to twelve inches. They were hanging it on the tree when grandpa came in. He not only had the silver weed, but had also found some sumac leaves that hadn't blown away. Grandma took them and put them in water till they soaked up enough so that they wouldn't break. Then she covered them in oil so that they would stay soft. The leaves were red, gold and a deep brown, and when they were hung on the tree it was just the gaudiest. When they were through, the three of them stood back and marveled at there work. The boy went and got his gifts and put them under the tree and then went and stood between his grandparents. His grandma put her arm around his shoulder, and his grandpa put his hand on his head, and the boy felt proud to be there grandson.

Christmas eve the boy was hard put to sit still.. He kept running to the window and looking out. When his grandma asked him why he was doing it, he said that in school his teacher had told them that on Christmas eve a fat man called Santa Clause came plowing through the sky in a sled and the whole thing was pulled by rain deer, what ever they were, cause the only deer he knew of where white tails and mulies. His grandpa said he had heard the same thing and lowed that it was true. This got the boy excited and he said he sure would like to catch one of those deer and ride it, his grandma said if he did catch one, it would take him up to the clouds and throw him off, and then she would have to patch him up and what kind of a Christmas would that be. The boy said he would hang on tight, and not fall off, but she said to keep his feet on the ground and that if he was in a sweat to ride something to go along and ride one of there cows. His grandpa looked at the clock on the wall and said it was past his bed time, and if Santa was to come he wouldn't come in as long as the boy was up, so the boy said he would go on to bed, and then asked if they were going to keep a fire in the stove all night cause if they did how would he get in. and started to worry and sweat over it, and his grandpa said that he was magic and he couldn't explain it, but that fire didn't hurt him and for the boy to go on to bed but it was a long time till he was asleep, and just tossed and turned till he was wore out and fell into a deep sleep that only the innocent enjoy.

11

The boy woke up before sun rise and went and set on the stairs to wait for his grandparents get up. He didn't have long to wait, they were both early risers. When his grandpa saw him sitting on the stairs he said that ever day ought to be Christmas cause if it was he wouldn't have to climb the stairs to roust him out. The boy was in fidgets to go to the tree, but waited till after breakfast was over and the whole tribe was together. He went and got his gifts and gave them first to grandma then to grandpa. He set on the floor and watched them open there gifts. His grandma was slow and deliberate. First she untied the twin and rolled it in a small ball, then she rolled the paper so as not to tear, and folded it up and put it aside. She then held up the shakers and the napkin holder and said that she had been looking at them for most of year and that they were the prettiest things a body ever did see and that she would prize them till creation. His grandpa on the other hand tore into his like a dog into a bone. He ripped the string off and then tore the paper to flinders and unrolled the belt with the silver buckle. Well I do declare, now if this isn't the finest thing. I been needing a belt and was hard put here lately to keep my pants up, if this don't do the job I don't know what will. Many thanks son, many thanks.

His grandma got up and went into the kitchen and came back with some cookies and a fresh pot of coffee and three cup. She poured the coffee and passed out the cookies and they had a merry old time. Soon his grandpa go up to go do the milking and when the boy started to go with him was told that it was to cold for him and to just stay in the house with grandma for now. The boy followed his grandma into the kitchen and watched her fill the salt and pepper shakers, and then she dug out some prize napkins that she only used on birthdays and Easter and put them in the holder. When she set it all on the table she said it just made the whole room brighter and that she was pleased as punch, and how that they were only for looking at, and any one caught touching them would get a thimble lump on there head. The she went on about her chores, but would stop ever now and then come look at her treasures and smile and be happy.

When grandpa came in he called out for a grandma and the boy to come see what he had found. Said he found it on the ground outside the house and it must have been dropped during the night cause it wasn't there last evening. It was a long narrow cardboard box and felt heavy. Grandpa said it might belong to the boy cause he didn't have much truck with boxes and the boy was always playing with them so he might as well have it. The boy opened one end and stuck his hand down into the box. He could feel something cold and hard, so he took hold of it and pulled it out. To his amazement it was a 20/2 single shot rifle, and there was even a box of shale's to go with it, well now...would you look at that his grandpa said. A new rifle, and all the fixing to go with it. Say now you don't suppose that old fat man dropped this out here on his way by? I'll just bet he did. Our chimney ain't the biggest and maybe he couldn't get down it, so I guess he just left it out here and figured we would find it.

The boy looked at it and held it and just had the fan tans over it. That old fat man sure did right by him and he lowed if he ever needed help all he had to do was sing out and he would come running. His grandpa told him that after lunch that he and to boy would go along to the orchard and he would show him how it worked, and they would get some shooting in. This was new hay for the boy, and he couldn't wait.

January came on with the cold renewed. It was the second Monday that the boy heard that his friend was sick. He heard that he might die if things kept going the as they were. The boy went down to his friends house only to be told that he was to sick to be seen, so he went back home. Later that evening his grandpa came in and said that he had been down at whities house and that he had died. He said he went quite and that they were going to have his funeral on Friday. The boy went up to his perch and set down and cried till he thought his eyes were going to come out of his head, this went on till he fell into a restless sleep. He dreamed that he and whitie were playing and that he turned and his friend was all white, even his clothes, and then he said that he had to be going and that the boy must check on his mom every now and then and the boy said he would and then whitie was gone.

The next day the boy went to whities house and saw his mom setting on a chair. She had her head bowed and was crying softly. The boy went in and walked up to her and she looked up at him and then he hugged her for the longest time. Latter after he left he thought over all that had gone on and he knew he would never forget the feel of whities mom crying onto his shoulder.

A week went by and grandma made a discovery. She came in the house and told grandpa that a new out house was needed. She said that it looked full to her, and grandpa asked her if she was the official out house inspector and she thumped him on the head with her bobbin and told him to get busy she went on to say one over flow and then they would be in a fine mess. Grandma asked if they could have a two holler like the Busshied did, and grandpa said he would think on it, and grandma rolled her eyes and said think on it, and went off muttering to her self. Grandpa and the boy went out to find a new spot for the out house, and the boy asked why they could not just put it next to the old one, and his grandpa said that if you did that then to much shit would collect in one place and might turn the water bad.

They found a good spot half way between the house and the hog pen, and grandpa said this will do cause when the wind was right you could smell the hog pen any way and when it blew the other way you could smell the out house, so he figured if he put them in the same area together then they would only have to put up with one smell when the wind was wrong instead of when the wind was wrong twice. They marked out a spot about four feet buy four feet and then staked it using four stakes and a string. Grandpa said as soon as the ground dried out enough they would get the whole business done in two or three days.

The soft warm breeze of April was like a tonic to the people in that part of the country. It had been a hard winter and they were ready for spring and summer. The wet left the ground slowly and the sun had a high old battle to get things dried out, but he stayed with it till the ground was clear of the puddles that had plagued the people. Grandpa said he was glad to see this winter pass and was looking forward to a day in the sun, and the boy had to agree. It had been a long winter, and it was good to see the giant white clouds floating against the light blue of the sky. They reminded the boy of huge cotton balls, all puffy and soft. He asked his grandpa if any one had ever touched a cloud and his grandpa said he didn't rightly know for sure, but he believed that they were soft and that some one had told him the Lord used them as a shield to hide behind so he could watch the going's on of the people on earth with out being seen. The boy said that made since to him, then got in a sweat and asked if he saw ever thing that went on, and grandpa said he thought so. This shook the boy up something fierce, and he decided that as long as there were clouds about he would be good so as not to get caught doing anything wrong.

A day or so before Easter grandma said they would all be going to a sunrise service. The boy asked what that was and she said it was when you went and watched the sun come up on the day that Christ came up from the dead. The boy asked if whitie would be there and his grandma said she didn't think so but he would be there in spirit. The boy started to badger her with questions and she got out of sorts and told him to quite pestering her and let her be about stuff she didn't know anything about, so he went and hunted up grandpa and asked him and he said the same, but lowed that if whitie was there it would be right and proper The boy went down to the orchard and climbed up in his tree and set for the longest time. He looked at the clouds again and then at the new buds coming on the trees. He thought about whitie and his grandparents and all that his last winter had brought about. He leaned back against the hard trunk of the tree and closed his eyes. He could feel the wind blow softly through his hair, and feel the warm sun on his face. He thought of Leeanna, and her dad and how he had made a friend of the principle. He thought of Horace and his fat mother and how much trouble he had with them. He more or less rehashed the whole winter and came to the idea that it had been a pretty good year even with whitie dieing and all. He set there the rest of the afternoon and on into the evening till the stars were out, then climbed down and went home.

12

It was half past four in the morning when grandma
rousted the whole house out. She said it was time to
get ready for the service and she would be dogged if they
were going to be late. Grandpa grumbled a little but the
boy was up and dressed in not time. This was going to
be new hay, what with all the folks that were going to be
there and all the fun he would have, it would be better
then when he got out at recess at school.

Grandpa went down and got the team hitched to the
wagon and said it was just more foolishness this sunrise
service, and the boy said it would give him time to catch
up on all the gossip in the country, so that cheered grandpa
up and he said it might be worth going to it after all. They
drove the wagon down to the house and grandpa got off
and helped grandma up to the seat and the boy got in the
back on the wagon bed. The morning was warm with
just a touch of a breeze and grandpa said he hopped this
wouldn't take more then a week to get through cause he
had chores and milking to do. Grandma said the chores
could slide for a little while, cause they were going to pay
there respects to the day that Christ a-rose from the grave.
Grandpa said she would pay respect all right if one of the

cows came down with udder fever from having to wait to long to be milked, she told him to hush up and just get along, and that everything would be ok.

Grandpa got back on the wagon and clucked the team into motion. Grandma was in high spirits about the coming service. She kept saying as how it would do them all good to get out of the house and see other people and grandpa asked her if that was the only reason she was wanting to go, and she got in a huff and said no, that it was a day of celebration, and if he was going to be put off about it she would go alone, but he said he wasn't put off about it just wondering if she was going so she could see the neighbors, and she said for him to just hush up and drive. The boy was looking forward to the service no matter what.

They arrived at the meeting ground at about five thirty. It was still dark and you could see folks coming from town and the lanterns from the country folk on wagons.

When the wagon stopped the boy jumped over the side to the ground, but grandpa got down and went around in front of the team and came up along grandma's side of the wagon. He held his hand up and she took it and then with him helping her keep her balance she got down to the ground. The boy watched as they stood looking at one another. His grandma seemed to look thirty years younger as she looked at his grandpa and his grandpa seemed to be a young man when he looked at her. They just looked at one another for a few moments then Miss Hap singer came along and called out Eddie, is that you. Grandma pulled away from grandpa and said it sure was, and what was going on. Miss Hap singer was the biggest gossip in Cherokee county, so she had a lot to tell. The two women went away, but the boy noticed that grandma kept looking over her shoulder at grandpa, and grandpa never took his eyes off her.

In the distance a bell started to ring to call the people to the meeting. A large cross had been placed in the center of the meeting ground. It was made from cutting down two pine trees and shaping them more or less till they were blocked and squared and nailed together. When grandpa saw it he said it gave him the shakes. When the boy asked why, he said well now. how would you like to be nailed to that and then stood up so's ever one could look at you? The boy looked at the cross again and said he reckoned he wouldn't. There was a woman standing next to them and she said she thought it was beautiful what with the sun coming up behind it and all, and grandpa said she would think beautiful if it was her hide hanging from it. She said he didn't understand, and he said he sure enough did understand. He went on to say that if the son of God hadn't let them hang him on the cross there wouldn't be no way he could ever pass through those heavenly gates those preachers keep harping about, but it still was a pizzen mean way to die. She looked at him like he just crawled from under a rock and flounced off. Grandpa said it did beat all he had ever seen how a woman could get her back up and think a man was dumber then a stick just cause he didn't go along with her ideas. The boy just watched and didn't say anything, he felt safer that way.

The bell had quite ringing, and the preacher had taken up his post at the cross. He stood for about one or two minutes with his hands folded and his head hung down onto his chest, then he raises his hands and head at the same time and looks over the folks all standing around, grandpa said he was looking for the best place to go eat when his yelling and screaming was done, and lets our a loud amen!!. Then he set in to telling the story about how Christ had died and went into such detail about it the boy started to get sick. He talked about how he was whipped, and how the blood flowed out of his back in streams. Then said some body came and slammed a crown of thorns down on his head and what a frightful and horrible pain that was. Next he told about how some roman drug this other feller out of the crowed that was watching and put him to dragging the cross. He told how when they got to a place called the skull they put Christ on the cross and nailed his hands and feet to it and how bad that hurt, and what awful pain he was in, and how he did all of this just so's the sinful folks of the earth could all go to heaven when they died.

The preacher had worked him self into an awful sweat by now, and had really got wound up. He sung into the part about how the sun went black at the moment Christ died and how the roman guard said that this was the son of God. He then went on to tell how at sun down when they came to take him off the cross that a roman stuck a spear in his side to make sure he was dead, and how blood and water came out of the wound. Next he told all about how he was taken to tomb a not far away and placed on a cold rock slab and covered up and then this big rock was rolled into place to keep folks out, and how on the third day the rock rolled away and Christ got up and came out of the tomb and defeated death and all.

While all this was going on with the preacher, there were things going on in the crowd. Some people were crying and holding there hands high, other's were on there knees praying and weaving from side to side, and some were shouting and jumping around. the boy was watching all this and trying to figure out what all the fuss was about. He looked up at his grandpa and found him looking at him. His grandpa took him by the hand a led him back to the wagon. He set him up on the tail gate of the wagon and thought for a moment, then he started to talk. He said what the preacher said was true, that Christ had died for them so's they could get to heaven and they must never forget all that he had gone through for them, then went on to say that the preacher only told part of the story, and that he had left out the part about that God loved us, and that was why he sent his son Christ to take on his shoulders the sins of the world so that he could pay the price for all them in one setting. He went on to say that in the bible Christ had at his command league's of angles, and if he wanted to he could have called them down to take care of folks that was causing all the trouble, but he didn't cause he wanted to die for the sin's and in that way the world would have a choice to follow him, or go on sinning, and end up in hell.

The boy thought this over and said he wanted to follow God and his son Christ, but some time's he was hard put to be good and his grandpa said it was the same with ever one and any time some one told him that he was going to hell, for him to ask to see there hands, and if there weren't any holes in them to just blow them off cause they weren't Christ, cause he was the only one who could say if you were going to hell or not. The boy said it sounded ok to him, then he and his grandpa went back to the meeting.

After the preacher got done hollering and carrying on, then the people split up to ear there Sunday breakfast. Grandpa got to worrying about getting his chores done and grandma told him to just hold up for a while, and then she looked at grandpa with that funny look and he did her the same way, and then he said he guessed the cows could wait after all. The boy was taking all this in when he heard some one call his name. He looked around and there stood Leeanna and her dad. Grandpa got up and invited them to join them for breakfast and they did. Grandma had packed a loaf of white bread and some jam, with some bacon and hard bold eggs. They all set in and ate like starved gentiles. After the meal Leeann's dad said it had been a while since he had a good old fashion breakfast, and the boy spoke up and said they ate like this all the time. Grandma told him to hush in the presence of grown up's and to mind his manners if he had any, and he said he did, but was hard put to find them just now, and lee Anna's dad just laughed and said he hadn't felt so much at home since his wife had passed away. Grandma asked how long ago that was, and he said it was right after his daughter was born, and grandma said it must be hard raising a youngen by his self and he said it was no bother at all, and that he wouldn't know what to do with out his little girl. Grandma said she would fix it so that they would get at least one good meal ever week and he said not to bother and she said it was no bother at all and then went to meet with some of her old cronies as his grandpa called them. His grandpa told him he had done it now, and that the good ladies of the town would be in a sweat to see that he and his daughter was well fed, even if it meant driving him crazy, and the principle said he could do with some good meals, and grandpa said meals yes, there company no. This put a new light on the subject and leeanna's dad started to look worried.

The bell started to ring again and all the people started to put up there fixn's and gather at the cross again. The preacher said a pizzen long prayer and then dismissed the people and ever one started to go home. Grandpa helped grandma back into the wagon and then looked around for the boy. He saw him standing with Leeann over by her dad's car, and called to him. The boy held her hand for a moment longer and then went to the wagon and climbed into the back and his grandpa started the team toward home. The boy looked back at Leeanna as long as he could see her, then set down and went to sleep.

The rest of the day passed uneventful for the small family, except when grandma went to find the boy to slop the hogs. It was his job, but it was one he hated, cause the hogs always made a mess of there food and the boy would get a funny feeling in his gut when he watched them eat. Grandpa told her he had already sloped them and she said he never, and he said he had to and she asked him to slop the hogs plenty of times and she called him a dunder head and he asked her why she was mad at him now, and she said it would take to long to explain, and left him setting at the kitchen table wondering what she was talking about. So passed Easter Sunday.

13

April left and may came in so's you couldn't tell the two apart. The breeze stayed warm and soft with fluffy white clouds floating over head. The robins and martins were coming back and the boy made up his mind that no matter what a bird did to him he wasn't going to do anything about it. He had had his fill of feeding birds and didn't want to have to go through that again, so he kept out of there way as much as possible.

After school one day he told his grandparents that there was going to be a school social at the end of the term. His grandma got excited and said that was just what they all needed, and she would be ready when it was. Grandpa said it was just more foolishness, but lowed he would go along to keep ma out of trouble.

The event was set for the last week of school, and ever one was invited. The boy said there was to be a school play and he was going to be in it. His grandpa asked him what part he was going to play, and he said he was going to be a Indian at a uprising, and his grandpa said that he didn't think to much of that, and when the boy asked why he said it was just more poking fun at the Indian and he felt that there had been enough of that to last a lifetime. Then he told the boy all of the amount of people that had died. The boy wanted to know if any of there family had been in on it, and his grandpa said that his mother and father were some of the first to have to make the march, and he didn't know why the whites kept dragging trouble for them then a one legged man in a ass kicking contest.

The boy said he wouldn't be a part of the show if that was the way it was and his grandpa said to go ahead and do it, so long as he knew that was just a play and not the real thing, so the boy said he would, but he wanted to know all about the trail of tears, so his grandpa told him it was nothing more then a land grab by the U.S. government and that those folks were in the same line of work as the banker's and the boy said if that was so then he wouldn't have anything to do with them, and his grandpa said it was to late, that even the bankers weren't as strong as the government, but that in some ways they were the same, and the boy asked how, and was told that only the politicians and the banker's could lie so much and still make you think you were getting a good deal. The boy went to the orchard to think about this.

The next day at school the boy asked his teacher about the trail of tears, and she said it was a bad time for the Indian, so the boy told her about what his grandpa said and asked her if it was true and she turned red in the face and said from one point of view it could be seen that way, so the boy asked how many different point's of view there were, and she got flustered and told him to let up on if for now.(Note) : two thirds of her class were Indian children, and looking back she may have thought that a new Indian uprising might take place in her class room. To be honest about it she was only thinking of her own hide at the time and what she said latter, could be forgiven.

The boy decided he wasn't going to get any where with her, so he just decided to do like his grandpa did when thing's got hot for him...SHUT UP.

At recess the other Indian children came to him and asked him to tell them again what his grandpa had said, and he did, but being a boy of not much experience, he got carried away and embellished on a few things so that when they went back in from recess there was almost an uprising. Even kids that were no more Indian then the teacher took the side of the boy, and the principle had to come down and talk to the class, for that matter he had to go to all the classes and give a speech. It was a while till the school settled down. It at the buss line that the tension finely broke. The boy was getting on the buss when he happened to look over and saw a big blond kids push a little Indian girl out of the way and she fell to the ground. She was not hurt, but the fact that it had happened was enough. He stepped aside while still standing on the second step of the buss and let the other kids get on. He waited till the blond headed kid started to step on the first step and then kicked him in the chest as hard as he could. The blond went back wards and landed on his butt. There was a surprised look on his face, which changed into one of anger. He lunged from the ground and grabbed the boy by the legs and pulled him to the ground. He was yelling dirty Indian, I'll kill ya, and the boy was screaming he would do the same to him. The boy got the whipping of his life, but gave of him self the best he had. They were scrapping around on the ground when a shower of cold water hit them both. that stopped the fight.

They looked up there stood the principle. He was the one who threw the bucket of cold water on them. He set the bucket down and asked what the fight was all about ? The blond said all he was doing was getting on the buss and this Indian planted his foot in his chest and knocked him to the ground. The principle said Hugh, then he looked at the boy and asked him to tell his side of the story. The boy told how he had seen the blond knock the little girl down and decided he would do the same to him to see how he liked it, and the blond denied ever doing it, then the girl he had knocked down came up and said he had.

The principle looked at the two boys for a second and then said for them to go to his office. As the boys made there way to the school he told the buss driver to wait that he wouldn't be long. When he got to his office the boys were on either side of his desk glaring at each other. He walked in ad told them to both set down.

First he looked at the boy and told him that the Indian wars were over, and that counting coop would get him know where, next he turned to the blond and asked him why he pushed the little girl down? He said she was a dirty Indian and he would push her or any other Indian down that he could find. He went on to say that Indians were trash, and couldn't learn come here from sick-um The principle set for a long time thinking. The boy noticed that his face got redder and redder as the blonde spoke. He finely said , so you think the Indian is stupid and cant think for there self? the blond said he reckoned so, and then the principle said he was Indian. One half Cherokee and he was not stupid. The blond said it would be about right for him to be an Indian the way he made over them and all. The principle looked at the blond for a long time and finely said, you know I have met people like you all my life, and I still cant figure you out. The red man was here before anyone, yet you think that just because your white you can dictate, control, and pass judgment on other? Well...in this school all are equal, and no matter if your Indian, white or black, you get the same treatment, no matter what.

He told the two boys to bend over, and he gave each one of them ten whacks with the paddle. Then he told them to go and get one the buss, and to quite making things hard on folks. The two boys turned to go, but the principle stopped the boy and said he wanted to talk to him some more. The boy turned around and went back into his office to a wait further punishment.

The principle came back in and set behind his desk and looked at the boy for a few moments, he then turned and looked out his window and started talking. He said people that were like the blond boy were sick. It was a sickness that he called prejudice, and there was know cure for it, but that a senator from Alabama had said just before the civil war. At the time there was a lot of fighting and arguing going on in Washington, and both politicians from the north and south were having it out, when this man spoke up and said, Gentlemen, if this cant be resolved here in these chambers, then I predict war, a hint to the wise is enough. He then set down and said no more. Well to make a long story short, the men weren't wise, and not long after that war broke out that almost destroyed this great nation of our's. Now let me conclude our little talk by saying that if people would just read there history before making decisions there would be less mistakes, now lets get you to the bus.

14

Lunch was over and the two walked down to the orchard and his grandpa set up some tin cans his , and a bar soap. He directed the boy shoot the soap first. The boy opened the bolt and put the shell into the breach, then he closed and locked it down. His grandpa showed him how to put on and take off the safety. He then took careful aim and squeezed the trigger. The gun made a cracking sound and before you could blink the soap exploded into pieced. His grandpa told him to put the gun down and then they walked over to the target. His grandpa bent over and picked up a few of the soap fragments, and turned to the boy with them in his hand and said " Now look at this and look close. If that there rifle gun will do this to a bar of soap. just what do you think it will do to an animal or a human being. ? That ain't no toy you got there, it's a man sized game getter. You never point it at any one, and always keep the safety on even when you think it ain't loaded. There's been more people killed by unloaded guns then you can think of, so don't ever take that thing for granted. When you go a hunting, only take a few shells with you, and count them before you start out, that way you can keep track of them. Never shoot at anything you can't see, and never, ever look down the barrel unless the bolt is out of it. Don't ever climb with a gun. Always set it down to go over a fence, and never play with it. Like I said it ain't a toy and it can be a friend to you, and put food on the table and protect you, or it can be the worst thing possible. You see that there gun don't know right from wrong, and it will do what ever you want it to. You have to be in control of it and never abuse it, cause if you do it can turn on you so fast your head will spin, and son when you make a mistake with a gun, most likely there ain't no taking it back."

The boy listened with raped attention. He took in everything his grandpa was saying, and made a promise to him self to always be careful and do right so as not to abuse his gun and loose the right to have it." One more thing I want to tell ya, and that is this. That gun will shoot straight, but that bullet will only go where you're a pointing. So never shoot up in the air with it. Cause what ever goes up comes back down, and that bullet is making tracks on the way up, and it's going to be doing the same thing on the way down. I remember the time when I was young. There was this family lived down the road a piece and the old woman was in the house fussing and bullyragging the old man when all the sudden she just falls over. He jumps up and ran to her and when he turned her over she was stone cold dead. She had a hole right between her eyes. There weren't no glass in the windows back then, and that bullet had come in through the window and killed her dead. It was found out latter that a man had been out hunting on the next place over. He had shot into the bushes trying to hit a running rabbit. The bullet missed the rabbit, but had went on another half mile and killed his old woman. So don't take that gun lightly, and always respect it and it will do you good." The boy lowed he would and then they shot at the targets a few more times and went home.

When they got home his grandpa showed him how to take the gun apart and clean it, and told him the names of all the parts and how they worked. His grandpa preached a little more about safety, and then they wrapped it up and put it away.

That gun was to become the boys greatest gift and latter on in life when he found him self down and out it would provide many a good meal. But when he got into some trouble with the police over something that was to prove out that he had been right and they were wrong it would be to late because by they had had plenty of time to get rid of the gun. He never got another like it, cause lets face it in ever boys life there is always that first gun and there will never be another one that will ever take it's place, just like your first car, your, first shave, your first bout with sex, or your first love. There are only a few first in ever boys life and this was one of his first.

December finely got out of the way and January came bouncing in with some more snow and ice, and the weather seem to take a turn for the worst. All the pounds froze solid and the boy and his grandpa was hard put to keep there's open so the cows could get to the water. It was on one of those cold gray days when the clouds seem so low that you could touch them and the wind was coming in fits that the boy and his grandpa set off to check the pound again. When they got there they could tell that the hole that they had been trying to keep open had froze up during the night. His grandpa took the ax he had brought along and walked to the edge of the pond. He tested the ice to see how thick it was and found it froze clear to the bottom. He turned and told the boy that they might need the sledge hammer before they were through, but that he would try to open the hole back up with the ax.

He balanced the ax in his hands then brought it above his right shoulder and swung it down with all his might. and glanced off, and a few ice chips few up and a small crack could be seen where the ax had hit the ice. His grandpa said that was a good sign and that maybe it was only froze to the bottom a few feet out. He took a few more whacks at the ice with the ax and said it must be so cause he couldn't see any water yet. He started to walk out in the ice and the boy said for him to take it slow that the pond took a sharp drop on this side and didn't go down a slant. Said he had found out the hard way last summer when he was fishing and had started to do some wading and suddenly found himself over his head and acting like a fish. Grandpa said he would and hit the ice again with his ax. There was a loud popping noise and a gurgling sound and the ice just seemed to drop under the old man.

He bobbed back to the surface in a second and the boy yelled for him to try to get to shore. His grandpa said he could not reach bottom and with all the clothes on was hard put to stay afloat. The boy asked if he could crawl out of the hole, and his grandpa said he'd give it a go. He brought both of his arms out of the water and laid them on the ice and tried to get his lower half to follow, but kept slipping back in. When he fell through the hole in the ice he had thrown his arms into the air and had let the ax fly out of his hand and it had landed on the ground behind him.

The boy ran over and picked it up and told his grandpa to reach as far as he could and he would see if he couldn't get the ax to him and maybe help pull him out. His grandpa said he was ni-froze and couldn't feel his legs and that if it reached his dingus that ma would never forgive him, and then he laughed.

The boy laid down on the ground and started to push the ax head end out toward his grandpa. He said for him to grab on to it and then try to get his legs out .Grandpa started trying to lift his legs out of the ice hole. He managed to get his right leg out and then worked till his left one followed. He scooted toward the boy till he was back on solid ice and then tried to stand up. He told the boy to give him a hand that his legs were numb and said he new how a chunk of wood felt now. The boy helped him to his feet and with his grandpa leaning on his shoulders they started home.

By the time they reached the house grandpas clothes were starting to freeze on him. When grandma saw them coming through the door she just had a Egyptian fit. She grabbed grandpa and pulled him in to the house and brought him over by the fire. She sent the boy for the wash tube and started to undress him . When the boy got back with the tub, she had grandpa down to his long johns and was chaffing his feet. She told the boy to set the tub down and to start filling it with water. The boy asked if she wanted the water heated up and she said cold water would be hot enough for now, so the boy got a bucket and started filling it with water. He filled the tub till it was half way full and then grandma told grandpa to get in and sit down. The boy thought the water would be cold when he set in it, but grandpa swore that it was hot and wanted to get out, but grandma told him to set or she would have him for sure, so he set back down and grumbled that she was boiling him and he now knew how a lobster felt what ever that was. The boy piped up and said it was a fish that live in the ocean and it had a hard shell, and his grandpa told him to quite being smart and showing off, and the boy said it was true, then grandma came in and told him to go hunting. The boy looked at her and asked if she was sure that is what she wanted him to do, and she said yes, that looking at him mooning around the house was more then she could stand and she didn't want to have to see his face till evening. The boy got his gun and counted out five shells and put them in his pocket. He went to tell her he was leaving and she asked him if he wanted her to hold his hand, he said no and she told him to get. On the way out the door his grandpa sang out he would like rabbit for supper and he hoped he could get one, the boy shouted back he would give all he had, and then closed the door. He hunted till it started to get dark and then went back to the house. He hadn't seen any thing to shoot and his grandpa said it was most likely to cold and he would have better luck when the weather warmed up but by then they would all be dead from the looks of the weather. The boy counted out his shells and was missing one then remember he hadn't unloaded the rifle, so he went and did it, then came back and told his grandpa about it and he said he had done right and that he would make a fine game getter and wouldn't worry about him and his gun any more, this made the boy feel grown up and happy.

After supper was over grandma sent grandpa off to bed and then started to heat water to fill up the red rubber hot water bottle. When the boy asked her why she was doing it, she said she was going to put it under the covers by grandpas feet, and he asked why and she was hard put to explain it but said it would help keep him warm and when he started to ask another question she got het up and said she would skin him if he didn't back off the questions, that she had enough on her mind and couldn't handle any more. The boy went to see how grandpa was doing and found him asleep, so he went on up to his perch and went to bed. It was past one when the boy woke up and wanted a drink of water. He got out of his bed and went down stairs real soft and easy so as not to wake up the folks. He got his drink and started to go back to bed when he thought about checking on his grandpa. He went to the door of there room and looked in. Grandpa was still sleeping but grandma was sitting up in her old rocker. The lamp was on but she had it turned down low and was sitting there with her head on her chest and snoring softly. The boy got a blanket from the foot of the bed and put it on her, and was leaving when she woke up and caught him. She asked him what she was doing and he told her, and then he asked how grandpa was and she said he had been chilling earlier but was resting quietly now. she went on to say that if it turned into lung fever she was going to have a fine old time of it and she said she make a pack to put on his chest. He asked how that would help and she said it would draw the fever out and when he started to say something else she said she had talked enough and if he knew what was what he would go and not pester her any more, so he went back to bed.

The next day grandpa was in bad shape. He was flushed and his skin was hot and he was coughing real hard and talking crazy. His grandma kept a vigil beside his bed and kept putting wet rags on him and praying and tried to get him to eat. The boy stayed out of her way. In the afternoon she came into the kitchen and asked him if he had got all the chores done, and he said all the milking was done and for her not to worry about it, and she said he was her man on the place till grandpa pulled through, and said again how much she needed the mustard, and the boy said he would go get some but she said it was to far and for him to go and not to worry his head about it, then she went back to where grandpa was.

That night he stole back down stairs and found grandma still sitting beside the bed and she had her eyes closed but the boy could see tear marks on her old she face and she was moving her lips and the boy knew she was praying. He went back to his room and got dressed. He then wrote a note to his grandma and told her in it that he was going to get some mustered and for her not to worry. He made his way back down stairs and left the note on the kitchen table where she could find it, and then went to the side door and opened it as slow and softly as possible. He went out the door and closed it gently behind him. It was cold. Colder then he had ever known it. When he breathed out his breath looked like a cloud and just hung. The stars were so clear that it looked like you could just reach up and pull one from the sky. He pulled his hat down over his ears and shoving his hands deep in his pockets then started off for town.

The snow that during the day had been soft, was hard and icy, and made for hard walking and he had to watch where he put his feet down to keep from slipping and falling down. He went down the drive to the road and turned right. He knew his grandpa needed the mustered, so there was no help for it but to get on with it and get back as soon as he could.

He was on the out skirts of town at day break. He had covered the eight miles in just under four hours and he said latter that a shadow had followed him into town and stayed with him till the sun came up and when he was asked what it was he said he couldn't be sure but thought it was an angle or something like that. When he told his grandpa about it he agreed with him and told him about how one time when he was younger he and some other men had gone hunting, and he had gotten separated and he had set down under a tree to rest and soon he had seen a lantern moving through the trees and he thought it was one of the men he had been with, so he called out to it and the lantern changed direction and came toward him, but when it got to him there was no one holding the thing it was just kind of floating about the ground. The boy asked him if he was scared, and he said not of the lantern, but was sure hard put to explain how the thing floated with no one holding it.

The boy went to the general store and was walking up when the clerk unlocked the door. The boy came inside and asked if they had any mustard, and the man said they did and showed him where it was. The boy got a jar of it and walked up to the counter. He said he would have to put it on his bill and the man said what bill you talking about, I don't remember you ever having one, and the boy said he would start one then cause he needed the mustered and wasn't leaving with out it. The man asked him why the mustered was so all fired important and the boy told him all about how his grandpa fell into the pond and now had lung fever and that his grandma needed the mustered to make a pack for his chest to draw the fever out, and the man said it was irregular and he was stumped if he could see how the mustered would help, but would go ahead and let him have it so long as he paid up the next time he was in town. The boy signed the bill book that the man had behind the counter and set off for home.

He was walking down the street when a car pulled up next to him and a man rolled the window down and said good morning. The boy stopped and looked at the man and saw that it was leeanna 's dad and said good morning back. The man then asked what he was doing in town so early and the boys said getting mustered.

Leeanna's dad laughed and said mustered, well where is your grandpa, and the boy told him all about what had been going on. When he had finished the man said " so you walked eight miles through this cold and snow to get mustered for your grandma to make a pack for your grandpa, and the boy said yes. The man said he had never heard of any one ever doing any thing like this before He told the boy to get in his car and that he would take him home, and the boy said it was ok that he didn't mind walking and the man said he would take him home any way and that if the mustered was so important for the boy to go through all he had, then his grandma would need it as soon as she could get it, and the boy said that put it in a different light and went around and got in the car on the passenger side of the front set.

The first thing the boy noticed when he got in the car was how warm it was and he said so. The man said it beat walking in the cold and snow, and the boy said you bet. The man said that he would have to be told how to get to the boys farm and he said it wasn't hard, and to just follow the road going east to the second mile section then turn left for four miles and when you came to Collins -Y- then turn right for one mile and then turn back left for another mile and you were there. The man said it was easy enough but for the boy to watch for him also.

What took the boy four hours to do coming into town, only took about thirty minutes or less to get back home. When he walked in his grandma was frothing at the mouth, and said she ought to thump him good forgoing to town like that but the mustered made up for it so she would forgive him this time. The boy took leeanna's dad in and showed him to his grandpa and the man said he didn't look good and grandpa said he felt worse but thought he would live. Grandma came in with her pack and told him to pull his shirt up so she could put it on his chest, and he said thunder-nation woman, you ain't going to pack me in that are you, and she said she was and to quite making such a ruckus in front of company, and grandpa said it was just terrible the way she was treating him and he was hard put to put up with any more of this business and wished she would go pester some one else, and that if it wasn't bad enough for her to try to drown him in a tub of water and then cook his feet all night with a hot water bottle, now she wanted to make a sallied on his chest and he wasn't going to stand for it. She told him to shut up or she would drag him back to the pond and throw him in again, and see if she couldn't finish him off the rest of him and that cooled him down some, but he grumbled and fussed about the mustered pack but she got it on him just the same.

The boy and his guest didn't say anything during the conversation between his grandparents, but when the walked back out side so the boy could tell him bye, they got to laughing and the man said it was the funniest argument he had ever heard and it was even better then radio, and the boy told him that he had heard them go at it even better and that if his grandpa had been feeling better it would have been ol'ned in there but right now he was poorly so it was mostly one sided with his grandpa getting the worst of it. The man (whose name the boy found out was C.M.Hill) said that he hadn't laughed so much in a long time and that it was better then a tonic to make a person feel good. He said he had to be going and the boy said to be sure to tell his daughter hello for him and he said he would. The boy watched the car go down the drive and turn right on to the road and then he went down to the milk barn to start his morning chores The mustered pack seemed to do the trick and grandpa was up and about in about a week. He said he still felt weak but would be back to full strength in no time. The boy said he was sure glad of it and had been doing all he could to keep the cows milked and all the chores plus go to school. Grandpa said the rest was a fine vacation if ma hadn't been such a trial, and just let him rest and said it sure beat all how a woman could act when a man wanted to just lay off for few days and take it easy, and the boy agreed cause grandma could find more for a body to do then he could keep up with.

That night at the supper table grandpa coughed some, and when he did the boy would mock him, so the two were just coughing and going on when grandma put her foot down, and said the next person who coughed in front of her would get a dose of the salts and a mustered pack, so the two decided to quite and be good, and grandma asked him why he didn't think before he did things like falling into ponds full of ice and grandpa said he could think, and she said not much further then his nose, grandpa got mad and said he could think all the way up to a county mile if he wanted too, but it put such a strain on him he would settle for just a few acres. Grandma rolled her eyes toward the ceiling and then back at the two setting around the table and told them to get out of her sight that she had had enough of men to last her a life time, big ones or small. Grandpa and the boy went down to the milk house and talked over what had been said and agreed that the woman half of the human race was just pain old ever day unpredictable and that they never would understand them if they lived forever.

15

After January had passed grandpa said he had seen some bad months in his life, but that this one had beat all he had ever seen and he wasn't in any hurry so see another like it. Grandma said it wasn't the month. But the fact that he decided to go swimming in a pond full of ice that did it, and he said he never did such a thing but that he fell in and he got in a huff and wouldn't talk for the rest of the day. Grandma said latter that she wished he would get upset more cause she had not had such a peaceful day since she could remember and said it was nice to have quite around ever now and then. After she said this the boy took off for the orchard and stayed out of her way.

The weather was still cold but it hadn't snowed for about two weeks and grandpa said maybe the worst of the weather was over and now all they would have to put up with was the infernal cold which in it's self was bad enough. It was Tuesday and the boy was waiting at the buss stop so he could go to school and as was his way he was thinking back over everything that had happened the few months and decided that trouble might leave them all alone for now, but wasn't about to take any bets on it. He was thinking all this over when the buss pulled up.. The door opened up and he got on. The buss driver by now was a full blown drunk, and had taken to packing a lunch pale, and had to stop ever few miles to refuel his tank. The boy said he smelt like a still and hoped no one lit a match around him cause sure as fire is hot he would blow up, and a blown up buss driver was more then he could stand. The buss ride to town was always an adventure cause you never knew if you were going to get there or not, and this caused a lot of talk among the children, so they all decided if they did get off in a ditch or stuck they would head for the nearest home and stay there and not worry about the buss or the driver who didn't seem to know what was going on any way. He was thinking about the time whitie had got on the buss and set down with the boy and asked him if he knew anything about Valentine's Day. The boy said he had heard the bigger kids talk about it but was hard put to make heads of it. Whitie had said it had to do with the girls and the boy wanted to know in what way, and whitie had said you had to give a heart to a girl with I love you written on it. The boy said he would like to know just what kind of heart it was and whitie had said it was one you made out of paper and colored it red and made it gaudier and mushier so as the girl would love it and keep it forever. The boy said it was just plain old foolishness and he would be stumped if he would do such a thing, and whitie had said he felt the same way, so they had agreed not to have anything to do with hearts and such and just let it pass. The boy was thinking all this and did not know that soon he would be the most sought after boy in the fourth grade.

They were half way to school and the buss driver had taken on quite a load, and was weaving all over the place when the buss got the best of him and he went into the ditch and up the other side. The buss took out about thirty yards of fence before it came to a stop. The driver set leaning over the wheel and was snoring to beat the band.

The boy got out of his seat and went up to him and nudged his right shoulder. The driver just smiled and belched and then went back to snoring. . After he laid him down and stood back up the boy noticed that one of the kids in the back of the bus was lying on the floor to. He went back to where girl was laying and bent over her. She had a bad cut over her left eye and was bleeding all over the floor. This scared the boy and he asked if anyone had anything he could put on the cut.

A little girl said she had a hankie and handed it to him. He put it on the cut and told whitie to hold it in place; he then went back up to where the driver lay. He tried to wake him up but he was out cold. A girl yelled that the bandage was almost full and the child was bleeding worse then ever, so the boy decided that he would just have to learn how to drive and quick.

He got behind the wheel and set in the seat. He looked at the peddles on the floor and tried to think back how the driver had worked them. He knew that one was for the gas, and the middle one was for the break. The other one he heard the driver call a clutch. There was also a button there that the driver used to start the buss. The boy put his foot on it and when he did the buss gave a lurch. Another boy walked up and said he thought that you had to move the stick that came up out of the floor to a certain position to push on the clutch in order o get the stick in to a position so that the buss would move and the other kid said he thought that that was so. He put his foot on the clutch and pushed. He had to hang onto the wheel to get enough pressure to press it down. He told the kids to try and move the stick into position and see what would happen. There was a grinding sound a clank and the stick went forward and the kid pushed on it. As the boy started to let up off the clutch the buss shuddered and the engine started to die, and he shoved his foot back down to the floor. Say now, how do you suppose he got it to go with out letting it die. and another boy spoke up and said you had to push on the gas at the same time you let the clutch up, so the boy put his right foot on the gas peddle and pushed it toward the floor, when he did the engine started to get loud and run faster, then he started to let the clutch out and the bus started to move foreword. The boy kept the pressure on the gas peddle and grabbed the wheel and before he knew it he had taken out about ten more yards of fence him self, but with the wheel firmly in his hands he turned the thing toward the road. The buss went back down into the ditch and climbed back to the road and at times was hard put to keep it there.

When they reached school they were late and the way the boy stopped the bus was to run it into a tree that was growing just off the school ground. The teachers and principle came running. When the door was opened and they got on the buss and saw all that had been going on, the principle picked the little girl up and carried her off the buss and put her in his car and left real fast. The teachers got the rest of the kids into the school house and started asking questions about what all had happened. There was a lot of excitement around the school in the after noon. The principle came back and said he had taken the little girl to the doctor, and she had gotten five stitches in her head and said that if they hadn't held the rag on her head she might have bled to death, and then went on to say that if it hadn't been for the boy getting the buss to town she might have died. He went on to say that the boy was hero and that the whole school could be proud of hem, and that he was the kind of boy that made it worth while to teach, and lavished such glory on him that he couldn't hardly stand it, and even the big kids said they couldn't have done better, and he had to tell the story over and over till he had about worn it out.

When school was over the principle took the boy home. They pulled into the boy's yard and got out of the car and went up to the door to go in the house and met his grandpa on the way out. His grandpa said well now.... what we got here? The principle told his grandpa how the goy had gotten the buss into town and might have save a life and how the whole school just thought the best of him, and his grandpa said he thought highly of him too, but then wanted to know who taught him to drive, and the boy said know one he had just done it on his own, and this shook grandpa to his shoes. He asked if was scared and the boy said not much, but didn't want to do it again. Grandpa said they had to go tell ma, so they went in and found her in the kitchen getting supper ready. Grandpa made her stop till the principle had told his tail of the buss and the little girl, and the boys grandma said it was just like a man not to think about what he was doing till he was doing it and that was probably the only reason he was able to do it. Grandpa said that what the boy had done was fine and why couldn't she be happy about it, and she said she was happy till they decided to hold court in her kitchen and go making a fuss over ever thing. Grandpa started to get into it with her and the principle said he had to go.

Grandpa and the boy followed the principle out to the car to see him of. Grandpa said it sure beat all the way ma carried on and he was hard put to explain it, and the principle said not to worry about it and got into his car and left. Grandpa and the boy went down to the milk barn to get the evening chores done. They didn't talk about what had happened, but the boy could tell his grandpa was wanting to ask about it. When the work slowed down some, his grandpa turned to him and asked, did you really drive that buss into town? And the boy said he had, then he wanted to know how fast they went, and the boy said he didn't know for sure, but they went faster then a team of horses could have made it. His grandpa said he would of like to of seen it, and wished he had, and felt bad cause he was left out of all the fun, and the boy said it weren't no fun trying to horse that buss down the road, and that he was hard put to keep the thing in the middle of the road, and his grandpa said he would of like to of seen it any way. The talk stopped there and they went on about there work, then went back to the house to eat.

The next day it was a different driver that had the buss and the boy asked where the other one was, and was told if he was smart he left the country because the parents of the kids that road the buss wanted his hide and if they found him he would be hung out to dry. The boy went on to his seat and set down. He was day dreaming when in his mind whitie got on the buss he came over and set down with the boy and said life just wasn't fair, and the boy asked him what he was talking about, and he said at school he was treated just like a hero, but at home he was treated just like something the dog dragged in and the cat wouldn't have and the boy said he knew what he meant, and white was for running away from home, but the boy said where could go in the dead of winter and be safe, and whitie said it was just a thought, but when spring came around he might take of till first frost, and the boy said yeah and in the mean time they forgot about you and then when you show up they act like they don't know you then where are you going to be. This shut whitie up, and they rode the rest of the way to school in silence.

By the time they reached school the boy worked his self into such misery thinking about how there family' had abused him that his spirits were down, and he felt like just going off some where and crying, cause nothing he seemed to do was right to here there folks talk and it was just plain ol'ned to have to toe the line all the time and not even be noticed, and then when you did something worth while to be treated like a dog, so he was feeling put out and down by the time the buss stopped. The first thing he saw when he got off the buss was the fat kid Horace push leeanna down on the school ground and then laugh. The boy didn't say any thing, he just walked up and kicked him as hard as he could on the knee cap, only thing is he missed the knee and got him in the privates. This folded Horace up like a fish worm on a hot stove. The boy was standing there looking at him when somebody hit him on the butt. He swung around and there stood Horace's mom the fat lady from the office. Say now. Why you want to hit me for the boy asked? You're picking on my little boy, and I won't stand for it, and she started to hit the boy again. Leeanna jumped on her back and started to pulling her hair and shouting that the boy was coming to her rescue, and that Horace was always pushing her down and being mean. There was quite a ruckus going on when the principle arrived. He broke the fight up and pulled leeanna off the lady, and told the boy to get Horace up off the ground and for all of them to get into his office NOW!!!!.

By the time they had all trooped into his office the fat lady was crying and said she had never been put up on so in all her life, and that her little boy was a good boy and that the other kids were just envious of her son cause he was so good looking, and the boy said good looking for a

Durham hog maybe, and she got mad and said he would have to apologize and the boy said he would be shot first and she said that could be taken care of, and the principle said for ever one to calm down and wanted to know what happened, so the boy told what he saw and leeanna said it was true and when the principle asked if Horace pushed her down he said he didn't mean to and that he was only playing and that the boy had no right kicking him in his private place, and the boy said he was going for his knee, but he moved so he got him in is pistol instead, and Horace's mom spoke up that was why she came to his aid, and the principle asked the boys if they remembered what he had told them last time about fighting and they said yes. The principle said he would have to give them all a spanking, and when the boy asked if Horace's mom got one to, this put the thing in a new light, and the boy reminded him that he said any one fighting would get the belt, and the principle said that was true so he guessed he would have to honor his word and told them all to bend over, and Horace's mom said she would not subject her self to a paddling, and the boy said her subject wasn't any more tender then his was and a good belting might do her some good, and the principle told him to be quiet, and he said he was only trying to help, and was told he was only making matters worse, so he shut up and vowed not to talk ever if that was the way they felt about it. Horace's mom said she wouldn't do it and would quite and take her boy with her, so the principle said if that was the way it had to be, then so be it.

After the mom and son left, one crying and one cussing, the principle told the boy to bend over and hit him twice on the butt, but not hard, and then told leeanna to bend over for the same and the boy asked if he could take her whipping for her cause he didn't think it was right for her to get a paddling and her father said no, that the punishment was the same for ever one, so she bent over and he gave her a couple of swats that were nothing, and then he told them to get on to class, so the two children left, and the boy asked her if she was hurt and she said no, then asked him how he felt and he said if that was the belting her dad was gonna give him, he reckoned he could stand about a hundred of them and then they laughed.

At lunch the story was all over the school about Horace and his mom and how the principle didn't spare even his daughter from punishment and this caused a lot of talk among the kid's both young and old. And they all decided that he was a fair and just man, even if he was a might hard.

If the story had spread fast in the school, it went like wild fire over the small town. Horace's dad went to the law and told him about it, and was told that any man who wouldn't spare punishment on his own, shouldn't have to play patty-cake with the help and to go on and leave him be. Horace's dad got mad and said he would see the principle and wouldn't let it lay, so the law locked him up for two days to cool him off, and when he went to let him go told him if he heard any more about this business he would lock him up till the cows came home, and Horace's dad said if this was the way that he and his family were going to be treated he would just move, so the law pointed toward the road and said he didn't care what he did so long as he let off the principle. Two days latter horce, his mom and dad and all there plunder had left town.

Some years latter the boy met horce again when he was doing a stretch in the U.S. Air Force. They didn't have much to say but it was noticed that horce stood with his hands over his privates when he was talking with the boy.

16

March first the rains came. It seemed one minute it was snowing and the next it was raining. The snow and ice melted fast from the constant down pour and it wasn't long till all the ponds and creeks were running neck full. Ever low spot on the ground filled up with water and there were even some out houses that filled to the top of there hole and ran over. The whole country started to smell like a pig sty. Grandpa said it beat anything he had ever seen and he expected to see Noah's ark to come floating down the road any minute the back country roads got so muddy that the dairy trucks that picked up the raw milk couldn't make there runs for getting stuck so ever one that was dairy farming had to load the cans full of milk on wagons and pull them to the hard top roads with horses. Ever morning and evening you could see between twenty five to thirty wagons sitting in the rain at the Collins-Y- waiting for the trucks that would pick the milk up and take it on to the processing dairy plant.

With the roads as bad as they were the school buss couldn't make it down them either, so all the boys and girls hopped a ride to the -Y- with there parents or some neighbor heading that way. Seemed like ever one was wet all the time. The boy observed he had, had more baths in the last weak then he had in his whole life.. There clothes were always damp. Another of his friends came down with the flu and died with in a week.

The boy felt lost, and alone. He went to the orchard and cried till he thought his eyes would float away. He had lost friends before, like when ol'ben had killed his last friend back last spring, but some how this was different. He could under stand snakes and such being what they were, but this was something else. He had just been talking with billie on Friday, and now Wednesday and he's in the ground. The boy was hard put to understand it all and felt like running away if this was the way the world was going to act, but then he calmed down and decided it was just more trouble, and this time instead of coming to him it went for billie.

When he got back to the house his grandma loved all over him and was crying and going on about how she loved him and hoped he would try to stay dry and not go out with out a hat on cause to lose him the way whities parents had lost him it would most break her old hear, and the boy said he would wear a hat and try to keep dry but it was going to be hard to do this with it raining all the time. She said she knew that but would worry about him all the more any way.

Grandpa was latter then usually coming back from is milk run, and the two of them were starting to get worried. The boy went up to his perch in the attic and watched out the window. About six he saw his grandpa coming down the road sitting high on his wagon seat. He looked ghostly coming in like that through the rain and made the boy shiver seeing it.

The wagon pulled up down at the milk house and the boy ran down stairs and told his grandma he was home, and before she could stop him he was out the door and going for the milk house. When he got there his grandpa was unloading five gallon milk cans from the wagon and setting them in the ice cooler. He ran up and grabbed him around the waist and hugged him. Grandpa the boy cried I been real worried about you, and so had grandma. Where you been ? Well now...I had to go into town to get something for you. Me? said the boy , I don't hardly need nothing. Well you need this I reckon and he pulled out a rubber looking blanket with a hole in it. It was green and smelled funny. Well , what is it asked the boy. Why now son it's what they call a poncho. You stick your head through the hole and let the whole thing hangs down all around you. It keep's the water off. Te boy looked at it and then he started to cry, and when his grandpa asked him why he was crying he told him if billie would have had one of these he might not be dead.

His grandpa took the boy by the hand and took him over to a hay bail and set him on it. "Now listen close to me, cause I got something to say and I'll only say it once, ok The boy nodded his head. We don't know when the good Lord above is going to call us home, we can only be ready to go when he does. Son there ain't nothing nice about death, but as sure as you born your going to die and there ain't now two ways about it. Life is a series of living and dieing. We ain't none of us going to get out of this life alive, but that don't mean we stop living. You see when we die we meet with the good Lord and he just takes us out of this old body and puts us in a new one in heaven. The body he gives us there is strong and never gets tired or sick. Right now your friend is in a new body and living it up. He wont ever be sick or feel pain. He will always be happy and not want for food. No, I'd say billie is doing right well by himself about now. One more thing is you got to think of is this, if old' Doc Cole was right, that boy wouldn't have been much use to his family or you much less to himself. But grandpa if he ain't much to us, how is he going to be much use to the Lord with his mind gone and all? Well now...in heaven everything is new. New body, new mind to I reckon. The boy thought about it for a few moments and said he would still like to have billie with him here, but that if the Lord wanted him, he would be hard put to get him back. His grandpa smiled his wise old smile and said he would figure it all out in time, but for now to just know that whitie,and billie was all right and he would see them some day in a better land.

Grandpa went on about his work with the cans and getting the horses unhitched, and the boy went back to the house. He didn't say much just went up to his room and set down and thought over all he and his grandpa had talked about. There were two things he had come to know as facts. One was that if you live your going to die, and the other one was that the ones left behind were the one's that hurt the most. He lay down and on the bed then and went to sleep, and in his dream he saw whitie, and billie playing and having fun and they didn't seem any worse the wear for his having the flu. He was in his right mind and talked plain as day. The boy wanted to stay and play with them but whitie and billie said they had to go, and he with the living for now, but someday they would all be together and then what a fine old time they would have.

When they boy woke up it was coming on to day light, and he felt glad and happy when he remembered the dream, and when he told the folks about it at the breakfast table his grandma cried and said for him to take care of him self again cause no matter how fine it might be at the other place she wanted to keep him with her here, and went off crying quietly in to the kitchen. The boy told his grandpa he was going to see Billie's folks this morning, and his grandpa said that was a fine idea.

After the morning chores were over the boy set off down the road in his poncho. It was still raining to beat all he ever saw, but the poncho kept him dry, or at least from his shoulders down. To protect his head he had an old felt cowboy hat his grandpa had given to him. It was to big so they had stuffed news paper around the inside of the sweat band to make it fit and that seemed to do the trick.

When he walked up in to Billie's front yard, he expected to see him come bouncing out the door, but this time there was no one to greet him. He knocked on the door and waited till his mom opened and told him to come in. She was the only one home at the time. The boy set down on a hard wooden chair and looked at her. she said she was putting up her lost boys things and that was the saddest time of her life. The boy didn't say any thing just watched. He finely looked at her face and got a shock. Her hair was all messed up and her eyes were puffy from crying. What wrinkles she had in her f ace seemed deeper, and her cheeks were wet. She left the room for a second then came back with some more of bellies things. As she placed them in the box she seemed to break down and started to cry with loud raking sobs. Her head was bent and her hair hung down over her face. Her shoulders shook so bad the boy was afraid she would shake her skin off. He watched her for a minute then got up and went over and got down on his knees and put both his arms around her and she turned her face in to his chest and cried and cried and cried.

The boy held her for the best part of an hour, and finely she got her self pulled together and set back and looked at the boy. She said he was a good friend and that billie thought the world of him, and she knew how bad he would miss billie even as his family did. The boy didn't say any thing he just set and the tears poured out of his eyes much like the rain that had brought the flu to his best friend. He stayed there for about three hours then said he had to go, but would be back latter in the week to see how she was doing, she thanked him and said he was a good boy to worry about her, so the boy left her and started back home, He didn't go straight home, instead he went to the orchard first and climbed up in to his sitting tree. He set and thought a long time about death and all the problems that can come to a person in there lives. He looked up at the rain falling through the limbs of the tree above him and them looked down at the ground. He tried to remember all his grandpa had said earlier, but kept seeing bellies mom's face instead. Then he remembered he hadn't told her about his dream. He jumped down from the tree and ran slipping and sliding back to bellies house. When he got there he didn't even stop to knock on the door and just went right in. He saw bellies mom sitting in a chair bent over with her face in her hands. She was crying again. He went over to her and got down on one knee. He put his small hands on her arms and softly told her about his dream, and his talk with his grandpa and all that was said. After he finished speaking the women set the way she was for a few minutes and the boy wondered if she had heard him. She slowly lifted her head and looked at him. She smiled and said that she had needed to here that, and she asked him to tell her again his dream so he did, and she smiled even bigger and said the boy had given her a new lease on life and that if billie was doing fine then she guessed she could to, then she hugged him till he thought his ribs would break. They then set and talked about billie and all that had gone on and finely when the boy had to go she said she was still sad and would miss billie but that she knew he was all right and wasn't hurting none, and that was worth ever thing to her. She hugged the boy again before he left and told him to be careful, and he said he wouldn't promise any thing beyond trying, and then he left.

Walking through the front door of his home he was thinking about how a few words could make all the difference in a body's life and went to talk with grandma, but some of the pigs had knocked down the pen and they were scattered to kingdom come, so she was in a bad humor when he got home, and thumped him on the head for leaving and not telling her where he was going, and he said he had told grandpa, and she said that was like telling a stump, and for him to get out of her way and go see if he couldn't help rounding up the rest of the hogs.

He found grandpa down by the pig sty herding the last of the hogs in to the pen. He told him how he had talked with bellies mom and how she said it made her feel better, and his grandpa said women put a lot in store with words and such, and that he was glad he had told her about the dream and all, that it might make her time of grief better, and the boy said he thought it would. Then they quite talking and the boy helped his grandpa mend the pen.

At supper his grandma brought up the business about him not being around when she needed him, and worked her self up into a fine row. The boy told her why he had done what he had done, and how it helped bellies mom, she relented some but not much, then set into grandpa cause he hadn't told her the boy was going visiting, and grandpa said he just hadn't thought of it, so she said it was a wonder he could even remember to put his pants on in the morning and he said he would never forget to put them on no matter how far his mind might wonder, and she told him to just put a lid on it, that with children dying and the rand and hogs getting out she was hard put to keep her sanity, and grandpa said it was true, and she started to cry and left the table and said she didn't want to be bothered by any one, and for them to just go and let her be, so grandpa and the boy went back to the milk house and went to bed.

Note: Whitie and Billie were a real boys, but in real life there name's were something else and has been changed for the writing of this book. The boy would miss them, not only in his youth but in his adult life as well.

17

September came in with out any fan fair, but the boy noticed that grandpa was being good. To good. Grandpa was in his hay day what with telling grandma off and all, but the boy knew it was to good to last. It was a week into the new month that grandpa came back from town with a surprise. He was real quite about what he brought home, and he had the whole tribe in a total fit of curiosity, and he was having the time of his life and enjoying him self all over the place. When he walked into the house with his prize under his arm, he held his head up and just looked at the ceiling and didn't even look at the boy or grandma.

Grandma jumped up and asked what he had in the tow-sack, and grandpa said she would find out directly, and then on through the room and on in the back part of the house. Grandma stood there first on foot and then the other, and then she starts to get mad. The boy who had just walked in and saw the whole thing and he was to laugh and laugh time after time about what he saw her do.

Grandma let out a howl that could of woke the dead if there had been any present, and then she set in to jumping around much like a Indian with his wigwam on fire, and just making the most wonderful kind of sounds, and then she went looking for grandpa and finely found him coming through the kitchen with a cup of butter milk in his hands and eating a slice of corn bread. She set in to him like a blue northern , and by the time she was finished grandpa was all wrung out. She told she was just as good as he was and when she asked a question she was supposed to get an answer and that if he felt him self to good to give her one that he could just get his own self and then went on to tell him a lot of other things and by and by and finely wound down to just calling grandpa and old rooster that had forgot how to crow.

Grandpa held both of hands up in front of him as if to fend off and attacking enemy, and then he started to laugh. He said why Eddie I didn't know you loved me so much. Now let me tell you something, I been wrong. I been gloating over having put you in you place and all. Now let me tell you what I got us. I got an radio. A genu-wine R.C.A. Victor radio. We can hear all sort of thing on it on Saturday night. I here tell there are a couple of guy's called ammos and Andy and I here they are a real laugh, not to mention little orphan Anne. I bet we have a lot of fun with this here radio.

Grandma put both of her hands to her mouth, and then she lets out a loud laugh and jumps on grandpa. She puts both her arm's around his neck and pulls his face down to hers and starts to kiss him all over his neck and then his face and then she just beams up at him and does the same back at her, and then they just hug each other till the boy thought they were going to cut each other in half.

Grandpa got his self dis-in-tangled from grandma and went and got the radio. Grandma stood there after grandpa left to get the radio, and then she laughed real soft to her self and said men.

The boy saw the whole thing and to this day he wondered what his grandma meant when she said Men, and then didn't says any thing else.

18

From then on, on Saturday night there was radio playing going on and the boy could only wonder at what he heard come out of the radio. There was all manner of music, and then there were the show's that his grandpa had talked about, and to the boy the radio was a source of amazement. He listened to the radio ever chance he got, and he loved the songs he heard, but most of all he loved the sound of the guitar and he would listen to the sound of the music till it filled him with a longing that he didn't understand but knew that some day he would, and then everything would be in place and he would be at peace in his soul. He wanted to learn to play the guitar, and he prayed to God to let him do it, and then he prayed some more. Always in his prayers he asked to be able to play the guitar and then he would go to sleep with dreams of him being the greatest picker in the world . Some how he knew that the guitar would be his best friend, and that when ever one else let him down he would always have the guitar, and he felt that, that would be good enough for him.

They boy told his grandpa how he felt about playing the guitar, and his grandpa said that the boy had a aunt that just played one to beat the band and if the boy was to ask her maybe she would teach him, and the boy said he would do it the next time he saw her.

The next day the Rawleigh man came, and he brought with him all kinds of things . He brought sewing thread and needles, and home cures. He also brought musical interments and books on how to go about ordering them. While the Rawleigh was showing grandpa all his latest wears, the boy was looking at one of his order books. While turning the pages the boy saw a guitar it was a harmony six strings with a solid bar neck. The boy looked at the price and saw that it cost all of fifteen dollars. He was setting there looking at the picture of it when his grandpa walked up behind him and leaned over his shoulder and took a look. The boy never noticed him looking, and after a few moments his grandpa walked away.

When the Rawleigh man was fixing to leave, the boy gave him back his book and said he sure wished he could have one of those guitar's and the Rawleigh man said if he could come up with the money, he could come up with the guitar and the boy said he would give it the best shot he had, and that he wanted the guitar with the -F- holes in it, and the man said he would do his best to get it, and they he said good by to the boy and his grandma.

As the Rawleigh man was leaving the boy watched out the window and saw his grandpa stop him at his car. He and the Rawleigh man talked for a few minutes and then his grandpa handed him something and then turned around and walked off. The boy didn't think much about it and figured his grandpa was ordering some more cow slave. The Rawleigh cow slave was the best that ever was. You could put it on cuts that a cow would get when leaning against barb-wire, or the cuts it would come up with when just walking through the grass. His grandpa swore by the Rawleigh slave and the marvel mystery oil. His grandpa would say that they could cure anything that walked, bar non It was about the end of September when the Rawleigh man came back by and he was real secretive and acted like he never had ever seen the boy in his life, and just walked by him and didn't even say hello or anything at all, and just went on into the house and left the boy standing in the front yard. After a few minutes of the boy standing there and trying to figure out what he had done to cause the man to act like that he herd his grandma calling him from behind the house. He started to walk toward the back of the house and then he saw his grandpa and the Rawleigh man come out the front door, and start toward the car. Well thought the boy, if he cant speak to me by my self, I'll be switched if I'll speak to him, and then he went on around the house and decided that he would let off trying to be nice to company if that was the way they were going to act.

When he got to the back of the house his grandma was no where in sight and he decided he was just hearing thing's and then he went on down toward the hog pen. The boy had discovered that hog's were right sociable critter's and that they could enjoy a good talk as much as the next person, and he had, had many a fine talk with them in the past so he decided to have one with them now.

He was just climbing up to the top rail of the hog stile, when he heard his grandpa calling for him to come to the front of the house. He thought well what do they want me for now and started to think his grandparents were playing tricks on him, and he was getting tired of running from the front of the house to the back and then to the front. He was thinking all this over and was starting to work him self up to being mad when he walked around the corner of the house, and what he saw just set his head to spinning, for there stood his grandpa holding a guitar. It was just like the one he had been looking at in the Rawleigh book and his grandpa and grandma and the Rawleigh man were all standing in the front yard looking at him and grinning like the three bears.

The boy let out a whoop and tore out for the three people, and when he got there he was grinning all over the place. Well now... said his grandpa, Look ah what I got here. I do believe it is something a certain body had been wanting and I do declare if he ain't got one now. With that he handed the guitar to the boy and said here you be son. Now I hope you can make music cause both me and ma sure do cotton to good sounds. The boy could only stand and look at the interment, and then he looked at his grandparents and then at the Rawleigh man, and all he could do was shake his head and say thank you, over and over again.

The Rawleigh man knew how to tune the guitar, and he had her all fixed up, and showed the boy how to do it, and then he showed him a few chords, and how to place his fingers and all and then he said he had to be running along, but that the next time he was by he would write down on paper the chords he knew and then the boy would have the beginning of a chord book, the boy could only stand and stare at the mans fingers as they played over the neck of the guitar, and was in a sweat to get his hands on it and start to play. He took to practicing two hours a day. At first it was hard on his fingers, and he got some blisters on the ends of his fingers on his left hand, but after three week's they begin to toughen up and then there were just calluses and the playing was much easier. He was setting playing some chords one day when the radio was on and he herd a tune called wild wood flower.

135

There was no singing just music, and he knew he had to learn to play that song. But where to begin? He new how to play some chords, but this picking was something else. He was hard put to get the thing going when his aunt came by one Sunday afternoon. She was by for a visit with folks, the boy cornered her and started to badger her about her showing him how the play the "ax" as his grandpa called it, and she told him to run get it and she would try to show him a thing or two, so he took off for his perch to get his guitar.

When got back down stairs his aunt was setting at the kitchen table talking with grandma and drinking a cup of butter milk. Grandpa was standing over by the kitchen sink just taking it all in. The boy walked up to his aunt and handed her the guitar, and she said it was the best one she had ever seen, and this made the boy proud and feet that he could do anything with guitar once he learned a few more thing's. His aunt strummed the strings and said the little E was out of tune so she tuned it up and then played a few chords, and then she turned to the boy and said for him to watch real careful, and he would learn a few things. the boy got a chair from the other side of the table and pulled it around so he could set in front of her, and she started the lesson. The boy was fast learner, and she only had to show him a few times how the chords, when played just one string at a time could be made so pick out a tune, and then she cut down on Wild Wood Flower. The boy's grandpa went to tapping his foot and grandma was tapping her hands on the table and the boy swore he had never heard any thing more wonderful in his life.

She showed him how to pick out the song and said that all he had to do was get the sound of the song in his head and then find the tune on the strings. She went on to play sugar foot rag, and then a Mexican tune that got grandpas feet to really moving. the boy took it all in like a dry rag and felt that for the first time he had a lot to learn.

After his aunt left he took his guitar back up to his perch and put it down looked at it for the longest time then went down to talk with his grandpa who by this time gone down to the milk barn and was getting ready to start the evening milking. When the boy got there he asked his grandpa if he could have a talk with him and his grandpa said why sho, and set down on a bail of hay. The boy thought for a minute then told his grandpa how much he liked the guitar, but was sure hard put to learn to play and wondered if his aunt had ever talked with him about it, and his grandpa said when she was a kid she had, had the same hard time learning the thing, but she kept on trying till she got it. The boy asked if that was all she did, was to just keep trying and his grandpa said yep, then his grandpa went to say that if a body wanted something worth while, then you had to work for it, and keep going till you got it, then he got up and went about his work and the boy thought over all he had said for a few minutes, then he turned and went to work to help his grandpa.

19

September came to close with the boy strumming on the strings and grandma and grandpa were all put back together again, and things just couldn't get any better to here them tell it. He also started back to school and was hard put to get to school and do his chores and find time to play his guitar. He complained about it one day his grandpa and his grandpa told him maybe he should start getting up an hour early so he could get in his time with his guitar and then he wouldn't be hard pressed to do everything else, so the boy said that is what he would do, so for the last three weeks the tribe had been waking up to the sound of a guitar instead of the rooster.

October came in with the trees starting to turn there many different colors, and the morning due was a might thicker on the grass, and the days started to get shorter, and shorter. The morning's were a bit cooler and the boy noticed that he was having to put more blankets on his bed at night, and it was the cold that drove him to keeping his guitar down stairs. School was starting to pan out about like always, except that whitie wasn't around to pass the time with, and then there was the fact that he was now in the fifth grade. He and his grandpa had made there usual trip into town to get his school clothes and while he was there he saw leeanna. She had sure grown over the summer and he said so and she said the same about him, then he asked his grandpa if he could take her over to the drug store and get a coke and his grandpa gave him fifteen cents and told him not to spend it all in one place.

When the two got to the drug store, they went in and set down on the high stools at the counter. The boy paid over a dime for the two cokes and a nickel for a bag of chips. Back in those dear dead days that is all a un-official first date cost, and the two were setting there catching each other up on all that had gone on over the summer. Leeanna told the boy all about going with her dad to visit some kin over in Mississippi, and the boy looked on in wonder as she talked about the Mississippi river being a whole damn mile wide where they had crossed it. The boy told her all about getting a guitar from the Rawleigh man, and leeanna said they didn't show with him much but did do business with the jewel-t man who cottoned to the townies. They were setting there talking when the boy's grandpa came in.

Grandpa didn't let on that he hadn't seen the two kid's but went on over and started talking with one of his cronies. The boy wasn't paying much attention to what was going on till be heard his grandpa up and say real loud, well now.., I reckon my grandson can just about play anything he wants on that guitar he has, and I am willing to bet you fifty cents to a dollar that he will at the next barn dance. The boy started to feel sick all of the sudden, then he looked at leeanna and saw her setting there smiling at him like he was made of gold, so he just kind'a swallowed hard and smiled back. Thing's might have been ok with what all had been said but then his grandpa went on to say that maybe the boy might even join up with the cow-bell's, which ever one knew was the local band that played at all the parties, and get together's the boy felt his heart sink to the bottom of his feet and then he looked at leeanna again and she was looking at him in wide eyed wonder and that just made him feel even worse. Duran, he thought, couldn't grandpa keep his mouth shut, and just leave well enough alone, and quite going on about him playing the guitar, and now to make matters worse he was telling the whole town he could play anything on it and he knew he could barely play three chords. He was thinking these thoughts when he here's one of grandpa's old cronies sing out that there is going to be a dance next Saturday night at the town hall and that grandpa could put up or shut up about the boy playing the guitar, by having him there to give a little tune for them all. Grandpa didn't even slow down, he just sailed right on to say that the boy would be there, and he would have enough money to back his play, and that any one who thought he was a piker would see it by then. The boy almost fell of his stool.

On the way home the boy lit into grandpa with both barrels. He asked him how he could do such a thing with him not even good at playing the chords, and his grandpa said he just thought the boy could use some gen-u-wine inspiration. Inspiration yes, shouted the boy but your going to make me the laughing stock of the whole town, not to mention the county, and then he settled down in a huff. Grandpa drove along for about another mile and then he said kind' a absent like, well now...if I was going to have to get up on that stage in front of the whole town, I do declare if I wouldn't be thinking of a way to get the job done, and then he didn't say any thing more.

When they got home the boy went right in and got his guitar and then he went up to his perch. He didn't say anything to grandma and she took that as a personal kick in the teeth and started up the stairs to tell him so when grandpa stopped her and told her all that took place. Grandma didn't say anything but got real thoughtful for a minute or two and then nodded her head up and down and said I might just work at that. The boy did not come down to supper, and at bed time and his grandparents were going to bed, they could here some where way up high the sound of a guitar being played and darn if it wasn't the beginning of Wild Wood Flower. The two old folks looked at each other and grinned and then lay there heads down and went to sleep.

the boy played long into the night and it was about four in the morning that he finely played the song all the way through. He was proud of him self, and when he went to bed he wasn't to worried about playing in front of the crowed, but was still some what put out with his grandpa. It was at breakfast that he told his grandparents he could play wild wood flower, and his grandpa said well now...get it out and let us here you pick some, but the boy said he would here it when ever one else in the county did and not one second sooner. His grandpa said that, that didn't seem right, but the boy said that his grandpa had set the rules, so now he would just have to live by them. His grandpa just laughed and said he guessed the boy was right and for him to run along to school, and he would be only to happy to wait till he could show him off at the dance.

20

When the boy got on the buss he went over and set down in his seat. He was setting there looking out the window and just wondering where all this would lead, when he heard some one telling some one to move out of there seat. He looked around and there stood this kid, and the kid was talking to him.

The boy looked at the kid for a minute and then turned back to looking out the window, and that is when the kid hit him on the arm and told him again to get out of his seat. the boy was trying to be nice, and didn't rally want any trouble but getting hit was to much. He looked up at the kid and said I was setting here first and I ain't moving. Now why don't you go find your self another seat and then ever one will be happy ? The kid looked at the boy and then said, "I don't want another seat. I don't want to set next to any boy or girl for that matter. the boy stared at the kid and then he said " say now...where you come from,? I don't remember seeing you last year or for that matter any time in my life.? The kid told him that his family had just moved out from down town Tulsa, and he was mad about having to be around low life's from the country, and the boy came back with that he had said just about enough, and that is when the kid slapped the boy across the face. The boy came unglued and he up's and whapped the kid up the side of his head, and when he did the kid fell the full length of the buss isle, and just lay there.

The rest of the kids just looked on and didn't say anything, they all felt that the kid had got just what he was asking for, and they all new not to push the boy, cause it didn't make any difference how big or small you were, if you got on his bad side he would just jump in with both feet and let the chip's fall where they would, besides the boy was one of them and not some up town pecker wood.

When the buss got to school, all the kids started to get off the buss and the kid on the floor hadn't moved a muscle since the boy had laid him out. They all had to walk around him or step over him. When the boy started to step over him the kid turned like a robin on a June bug, and grabbed his right leg and bit him in the calf the boy yelled and then he fell to the floor of the buss. The boy fell on his face and before he could get turned over the kid had landed on his back and was pressing him down and trying to choke him all at once. The boy was hard put to take anymore and kept struggling, but the kid was riding him like a horse, and no matter which way he turned the boy went with him. Pretty soon the kid's left arm came in front of the boy's mouth and the boy opened his mouth and sunk his teeth to the bone. The kid screamed like a girl and started to try to tear his arm from the boy but the boy hung on like a bull dog and just kept chewing. Pretty soon the kid gave a hard jerk and got his arm free, but at the price of loosing a hunk of hide, hair and all. He was bleeding like a stuck pig and screaming worse then a girl, he fell back off the boy and that was all it took. Once the boy was free he got up on his hand and knees and when he looked down through his legs he saw the kid setting there crying and holding his arm, so he just played like a mule and kicked back with his left leg and caught the kid on the edge of the chin and that stopped his screaming cause the kid's eyes just kind of glazed and then he fell over on his back. There Duran your crusty hide, I bet you leave me alone now.

The boy was just getting up when the principle came stepping onto the buss. Say now what is going on now, he asked, and the boy told him the story, and the buss driver backed him up and so did the rest of the kid's so the principle told him to go on to class and he got the kid up and went over and put him in his car and left. The boy wondered if the same rules would be applied as last year, but didn't worry to much about it, he would take a licking ever day if it meant keeping a leg biting dog that posed as a person off him.

It was right after lunch that the principle called the boy to the office. When he walked in there set the leg bitter, and he was not alone. A big man was setting next to him and the boy knew that this had to be the boy's dad. The principle asked the boy to be seated and the boy went around the desk and set as far away from them as he could. the principle started the talk by way of introducing ever one. the boy found out that the man's name was Mr. Hug, and his kids name was Leroy. Mr. Hug was an ex-banker that had got tired of the rat race as he put it in Tulsa and had moved to the country for some peace and quite. He went on to say that he would like for the boy's to be friends, and how that ever one should get along and not be causing trouble and all. The boy listened with only half and ear, but his eyes were on the Hug. He found out that the Hug couldn't meet his eyes so he knew for sure that this ex-pain in the ass was a real frog choker, and he decided that as the man wound down and quite making speeches that he would have his say and be done with it and let it fall where it would.

When after about thirty minutes of the Hug running his mouth in typical banker fashion he finely shut up his clap-trap and the boy had his say. He told the Hug that the only way he would be a friend to his kid would be if he was dead. He went on to tell the banker and his kid what he though of banker's and there kin. When he finished up with one last put down, he shut up and vowed to him self he would be skinned alive before he said another word. The principle was having a hard time to keep a straight face, but he did a good job of it, and only after the Hug and his kid left and the boy went back to class did he break down and laugh. He thought again how one honest answer could dispel a whole tub full of non-sense, that the boy had called a raft of bull shit, bar none.

The Hug took to driving Leroy to school so his dainty little butt wouldn't have to set next to the low lives, any way that is the way the boy put it. The boy didn't have any more trouble from the Hug or his Kid. They moved back to Tulsa after living in the country for only a few months. You see after the folks around there found out he was a banker and a blow hard to boot, they just clammed up and wouldn't talk to him, and the stores in town would always make him wait till the very last to be served, and to top it all off, not one person was impressed by him. The boy's grandpa said latter that the country was no place for a soft handed money grubbing, back biting, pain in the ass to be. He said this in the drug store, and Duran if there was no one who would argue with him. Grandpa finely struck a subject that the whole town agreed on.

The night of the dance went pretty good and the boy got up and played Wild wood flower, and then ghost riders in the sky, and the folks all said he did a prime job of it and grandpa came out about six dollars a head, an the boy become the talk of all his class mates, and best of all leeanna thought he was the best. The rest of September went by with out much more going on, except the boy learned one thing, and that was, when your put to the test the best way to get by was just dig in and do your best and God and time would work ever thing out ok.

21

October was a bust. The boy was having a good time playing his guitar, and going hunting for game and such, but he was lonesome. Last year whitie had been around to do thing's with, but now there was no one to share things with, so what did it matter if you did something great, and felt real good about it. It didn't mean rock's if there wasn't some one to share it with. Soon the boy just about quite doing any thing and his grandparents started to worry about him, and they had many a long talk at night after the boy went to bed about it, but they were stumped as to what the trouble was.

Grandma tried to find out by detective work. She would drop sly questions and look to see how the boy would answer, but he either said nothing or just passed them off. This got her more perplexed then ever and she started to wonder even more what was wrong. It was grandpa who finely figured out what was wrong, and he came about it by accident.

The boy was down at the hay barn just mooning around and didn't see his grandpa come walking up. His grandpa started to speak when he heard the boy talking. Now who is he talking to. He wondered. As he got closer he saw that it was only the boy talking to him self and he started to turn away when he caught the words, "Damn whitie, why did you have to die?" It sure is lonesome around here with out you, and I got so much to tell you and do with you, but you had to go and die just when thing's were starting to get interesting, and with that he just hung his head. His grandpa saw the whole thing, and started to say something but he decided to just let it lay. Some thing's a body had to work our for there selves, and he knew when the boy felt like it he would come and talk with him, but till then he would say nothing, nor let on he knew how the boy felt.

Grandpa went back up to the house and told grandma what he had learned and she said she could understand it, but was hard put to know what to do about it all . Grandpa said he guessed the best they could hope for was that the boy would find another friend and then maybe things would get back to normal for him, and grandma said she would pray about it and grandpa said while she prayed he would just hump along and see what he could come up with and that maybe that between her getting after the good Lord and him smooching around they might come up with something.

About a week before the night of Halloween, grandpa got an idea. He went and talked it over with grandma, and she said it might work and for him to give at a go, so he said he would and that it might just do them all a world of good, and grandma got all excited and was hard put not to tell the boy what was up, but vowed she would keep her mouth shut till creation, and grandpa told her she better for all there sakes, and grandma said she could keep her trap shut as good as he could, and they got into an argument and was going at it hot and heavy when the boy came down from his perch and asked them what was going on, and grandma being mad almost spilled the whole thing but caught her self and had to leave the field of battle with a well known loss. When she look back grandpa was standing there smile'n at her and she vowed to her self that she would get him that night after the boy had gone to bed.

The next day after the boy had gone off to school, grandpa set about getting the dance all lined out. First he called the leader of the Cow Bell's and made arrangements with him for the music, then he called up the paper and put a big ad in it telling all about the dance and where it was to be held and when. Then he and grandma set down and started to plan the food and drinks that were to be served. Grandma said there would be no drinking and grandpa said ah shucks now a little hard cider never hurt any one, and grandma said the cider didn't but a rolling pin would and grandpa decided that if there was to be any drinking around the place it would have to be out back where the hog's lived.

By the time the boy got back from school the plans were laid and ever thing was in order. Grandpa hinted that the boy better start to learn some new tunes on his ax and when the boy asked why his grandpa shut up tighter then a rusty hinge and wouldn't say another word. The boy knew something was up by the way his grandpa was acting, so he went to talk with his grandma, but she was busy and didn't have time to talk so he went on down to the milk barn and started his chores. As he worked he was thinking about how some folks could sure change. Now take for instance what went on at school that very day. You would of thought that ever thing was going to be ok, and then just for no reason at all he was called to the principles office, and when he got there he had to wait for about fifteen minutes, and when the principle finely showed up he said it was just a mistake and for him to go on back to class, but when he got there everyone acted like he had lice or something and no one would even speak to him, not even leeanna. His whole day was a pure bust, and he swore that if things kept up he would just pack his grip and make tracks for better parts, where ever that was.

What the boy didn't know was that his grandpa had also called the school and told the principle about the coming shin-dig, and wanted him to tell the school, but the boy was to know nothing about it. The principle told him he would take care of it, and for him not to worry, grandpa said he wasn't worried about the countries, they knew how to keep there trap's shut but it was the townies that had him shook, but the principle told him that if any one told the boy and he found out about it he would hide and heel them out of the school in nothing flat. That made grandpa feel better.

The principle said to back his play had called the high sheriff and asked him to come to the school and when he asked him why the principle told him he wanted some support in the matter, so the high sheriff came over and while the boy was waiting in the principle's office, the principle and the high sheriff were making the rounds of the classes, and spreading the word, as well as a warning, and it only took the high sheriff's face to make ever kid in school feel like they had lock-jaw where they boy was concerned.

After the boy finished his chores he went back up to the house to wash up for supper and then he went to find his grandpa, but couldn't turn him up, so he hunted down his grandma and found her down in the cellar picking out the can goods for supper. Say now grandma I got to Talk with you, and she was in to much of a hurry to get supper on and for him to go bother grandpa, and he said he had tried to find him but couldn't and was hard put to talk to some body, and grandma said she wasn't the some body he was looking for and then she went up the stairs out of the cellar and went into the house.

The boy felt low. he went down to the hog pen to see if they wanted to have a talk, but the hog's were all eating and didn't seem to be in a listening mood, so he decided he would just go down to his orchard and talk with the tree's and as far as he was concerned the rest of the tribe could go and stay put.

While the boy was down at the orchard his grandpa came in and grandma told him about her talk with the boy and his grandpa told her not to worry none that it would all work out and then she would see that he was right and be happy Grandma said he might be right but she would have to think about being happy, and grandpa just laughed. The rest of the week passed fast and soon it was the night of the dance. Grandpa sent the boy down to the milk barn to clean up as he said. The boy was down there when the people started to arrive. The band was the first to get there, but they had no sooner showed up till the rest of the in-vitas, as grandpa called them started to show.

The boy was finishing up with a last load of cow-shit in his wheel-barrow, when his grandpa walked in and told him to get up to the house pronto. Now what thought the boy as he started to walk toward the house he could hear music coming from inside the house. He started to get excited. A party. They were having a party and by jing's it was a surprise one at that. When he walked into the house the first person he saw was the principle and his daughter Leeanna. Leeanna walked over to him and took his hand and smiled at him and he got red in the face, or as red as an Indian can ever show, and smiled back at her. The music being played in the back ground was a country tune called Dooley, and it would fair set your feet to moving, and to watch the people dance reminded the boy of a bunch of ant stompers at a pick-nick.

When the song ended the band leader called out to the boy to go get his guitar and get up there and join them, so he went and got it, and feeling very self conscious, stepped up on the little put up stage with the rest of the band. They played Old Jim Miller, Wild wood flower, Fire ball mail, Precious memories, Blue yodel number 9, Mule skinner blues, and whole lot more The boy was in his hay day. He said latter he hadn't had so much fun since he and whitie had pushed over all those out house's, on last Halloween. His grandpa looked at him when he said that and it was then the boy remembered that he had never told his grandpa about that, so he made a soft, if not fast retreat from his sight for the rest of the day.

The dance lasted till almost four in the morning, and by then the boys fingers felt like they were about to fall off his hands. Most ever body stayed on after the band shut down and went to sleep on pallet's on the floor or in there cars or wagons. Some of the men had already fallen asleep, but grandma said it was due to the hard cider out by the pig stile not because they were tired. There was to be a new sport that was to crop up among the men and boys after the dance that involved hogs, but that is another story so we won't bother with that right now.

22

October came to a close with ever one and there dog's happy and on speaking terms. The dance cured a lot of still hard feeling's left over from the quilting bee gossip trouble, and ever one vowed that they were going to have more of these get together's and some of the people even thought it was a good idea to have one ever month at a different person's house.

The boy was asked if he would become a part time player with the cow bell's and when he asked why part time, was told he could play at socials, but not in the bar's and the boy said that was just jiffy with him, cause he didn't cotton to bar's any, and went on to say that he had an uncle that was killed in one and he couldn't see that they were worth any thing but trouble and he already had enough of that.

It was three day's into November when the first winter storm hit, and it was a fish freezer. His grandpa said so. He said he was down by the pond when a fish jumped out of the water and while it was still in the air it froze solid and that water that was coming up with him froze too so as to make it look like the fish was jumping and never going to land. Grandma old him there were liars in hell same as crook's and grandpa swore it was so, and grandma said if it was true why didn't he just go down there and net him a few for the coming winter, and grandpa said froze fish was tainted and he would be dogged if he would eat one, and that only those of low charter would do such a thing, and grandma threw her hand's up and rolled her eyes toward the ceiling and just walked off, leaving grandpa still vowing to what he said was true.

The boy in the mean time had decided to give it a go at hunting turkeys. He got out his 22 rifle and checked it over as he always did before going out hunting and after he was satisfied that it was working ok, he got some bullets and told his grandma where he was going and set out. He was bundled up so he could keep warm. He had on a pair of long-john's and over these he had a pair of levis with two pairs of socks and his boots. He wore a red scarf, yet even with all this on he could still feel the cold maker and he shivered when he thought of him and how he had almost killed him last winter.

They boy set out for the bottoms. It was the same place just a year be for that he and whitie had, had so much trouble with skunks. It took him about an hour to get there, what with climbing over fences and falls into snow drifts, to say the least it was hard going, but when he made the trees the snow thinned out and the wind wasn't to bad. The first thing he did was to look for tracks, and there were plenty of them around. The boy started to move slow, and stop ever few feet to look all about. He went further into the bottoms then he and whitie had ever gone, but he was on the hunt and didn't pay much attention to where he was going. It was the turkeys making noise that alerted him to where they were, so the boy was going at a snails pace when he saw them. There was a whole raft of them all setting in the lower branches of a old black jack. The boy lifted his rifle and ever so slowly took aim. When he fired the crack of the rifle sounded loud in the stillness of the forest and the boy, even knowing it was going to make sound, jumped in spit of him self. The turkeys in the mean time took off in a rush of sound and feathers, that left the branches of the trees rocking and shaking like a great hand had been shaking he tree. The boy stood there for a second or two then walked over to see if he had hit anything. He had. It was a big old turkey gobbler, and his beard must have been seven or eight inches long The boy bent over to pick it up and found it heavier then he thought. It must weigh at least thirty pounds or more he thought, but he knew once he had gutted it, it would weigh less.

It had started to snow again when grandpa came up from the barn and walked into the house. Say now ma, where's chch at ? I ain't seen him all day and it's starting to get late. Well he went hunting and he should be getting back real soon, but I am getting a mite worried. She was a lot more worried then she let on, and grandpa knew it by the way she kept going to the window and looking out toward where the bottoms were. Grandpa fooled around the house for about thirty minutes or more then said he was going to go looking for the boy, not that he was worried or anything like that, but he might need help getting his game home if he had any. Was what he told grandma. She thought that was a good idea and said she would have supper on by the time they got back. Grandpa went down to the barn and saddled up one of the horses and was just starting to step into the saddle when he looked up and about died laughing, for here comes the boy and Duran if he didn't look like a half man, half turkey.

The boy had gutted out the turkey but even then it weighed about twenty five pounds or more and he was hard put to carry it, but had managed to lug it back to the road where he was just about played out. He set for about twenty minutes and then got back up and bent over to pick up his bird and that is when he saw the coyote, or better yet coyote's. There were five of them and they were hungry. The boy knew all about coyote's and how they worked, so he decided to just keep them in sight and move on down the road, and if they made a rush for him, he would let them have a good go for it. He jacked a shell into his rifle and started to walk. He didn't hurry, just took a easy stride, cause he knew if he fell down the coyote's would be on him quicker then the wink of an eye.

From where the boy had come out of the bottoms and back to his home it was about four mile, and the coyote's stayed with him all the way and it was only when he turned in to the drive going down to the house that they let up following him, you see the coyote's knew all about grandma and her shot gun, and knew it was best to steer clear of that part of the country.

Grandpa walked up to the boy and relieved him of his burden and was as proud of the bird as if he had got it him self. he was yellowing for ma to come and see and slapping the boy on the back and just having jigger fit's all over the place. Grandpa came out and said it was a nice bird but that if he was going to be going around a worrying the whole tribe with his hunting she would be hard put not to scalp him.

Grandpa said for her to just go along and let a man be, that when ever a man had done something like the boy had done that he should be praised and done over and not harped on, and grandma said she praised God, not man as far as that went she had got a turkey last year by just being smart and not causing a whole lot of worry and ruckus. This got grandpa mad and he started to try to lay down the law and the two of them were going at it hot and heavy. The boy stood back and watched them. He saw where there were tear stains on grandma's old cheeks and he had seen the relief in grandpa's face when he came running up and he knew that this was just there way of letting the worry get out of them. He laid down his rifle and walked over to his grandma and put his arms around her and hugged her with all his might. He then looked up into her wise ole eyes and took in the wrinkle on her face as well as the gray hair that was always done up in a neat bun on top of her head and said " I love you grandma and didn't mean to worry you none. " She looked down at the boy and then she bent and kissed him on top of the head and told him to run along and pluck the bird and that when thanks giving came they would have a feed to set the pilgrims back." and then she turned and hustled for the house wiping her nose and eyes with her hand.

Grandpa and the boy went on down to the barn to pluck the bird and grandpa made the boy tell all about the hunting and how the boy had stalked the bird and then the trip back home, and the boy told him the more he talked the brighter grandpa's eyes got and by the time he was finished grandpa was in a sweat, and told the boy so, then went on to say that what the boy had done many a man couldn't have done it, and this made the boy proud and he felt more like a man then ever and grandpa told him that he had all the equipment to be called a man, and when the boy asked him what that mean, his grandpa said ever time he took a leak he held it in his hand and the boy asked if that was what made a man and his grandpa said it was a good starting point, and as he grew he would learn more and more about how to be one, and it was up to him if he wanted to be a good one or not. The boy thought about this for a few minutes and then asked what a good man was like and his grandpa said he would have to find that out for him self, but the best way to do it would be to just let his heart and God guide him to do what was right and if he did that he would never go wrong.

About that time grandma called out and asked if they were finished and the talk stopped. The boy thought more and more about what his grandpa said and decided to do like he said that night in his prayers he asked God to guide him and help him do right. This was to be something he always put in when ever he talked with God. The boy didn't talk with God to much unless it was real important. He felt that the Good Lord above was in a sweat to run the world and keep down trouble and he didn't want to bother him to much, but he always knew he was there to talk to, also he had the idea that if you kept asking for things all the time that God would get tired of trying to sort out what it was you really wanted and just put the whole thing on hold, no, it was best to just go and talk with him when you needed something, and then let God guide you the rest of the time, and if you were living your life the best you could and following the Good Book and what it said to do, God would back you ever time, but it was best not to clutter up his ears with a bunch of useless talk.

They got the bird plucked and then took him up to the house but not before grandma had weighed it on the milk scales. The bird dressed out at 22 and pounds. Grandpa said it was a prime bird and that he couldn't hardly wait to sink his teeth into it, the boy agreed.

At the house they turned the bird over to grandma who then took it and put it in a tub full of water that she had got ready for it. She had put in salt and pepper and some sage. She would soak the whole thing over night and the next day she would take it out and then insert small pieces of butter under the skin all over the bird then she would wrap it all up and put in the ice house till the day before thanksgiving. She came in and told the boy it would be the best turkey ever and she was real proud of him and then she asked him if he would like to invite leeanna and he dad to take thanksgiving with them and he said he would sure ask them, and that was how the boy and his girl got together for there first holiday.

Thanksgiving morning the house was all in a up-roar. Grandpa had got up earlier then usual and he and the boy had got the morning chores out of the way as soon as they could. Grandma had been up since four in the morning getting the bird ready. She told them all that there was to be stuffing and corn on the cob, along with potato's and gravy. There world also be cranberries with some new stuff she called Jell-O. There was to be apple and cherry and pumpkin pies, along with all the peaches and blackberries jams that they could hold. She also said there would be fresh made bread with her special honey butter. The boy and his grandpa were fit to be tied when she told them that, and there stomachs were groaning all morning. By the time they had finished up at the barn and started back to the house they could smell the food and grandpa stopped and did a little jig in the snow and said it did beat all how a thing like the smell of good food could set a body to feeling so good he felt he could live for ever.

Leeanna and her dad arrived about eleven or so, and when they got in the house Leeann's dad said he would smell the cooking clear down at the Collins -Y-, and grandma said one old lair in the house was enough and that grandpa was it and he didn't need any computation in that area, and the principle laughed. Grandpa had been standing back and looking on, but soon he walked up to the principle and said something low under his breath

Norman W. McGuire

and Leeann's dad nodded yes, so grandpa took him by the arm and steered him out the door and toward the well house. Grandma was giving them the evil eye the whole time. Leeanna walked up to grandma and asked her if there was anything she could do to help and grandma put her left arm around her shoulder and said come on child well get the table set, but she kept looking over her shoulder after the two retreating men.

After Leeanna and grandma left the boy went out the door and followed his grandpa and leeanna's dad. He caught up with them down at the well house and walked up just as grandpa was un-corking a jug of his cider. His grandpa smelled the jug and got this big grin on his face like a fresh milked cow, and then he took a big long swig. When he took the jug from his mouth he sucked in a whole yard full of air and then blew it out. He then handed the jug to leeanna's dad who did the same and it was about then that grandpa saw the boy standing there. Well now.....The founder of the feast He says, here son I reckon you can take a nip to you earned it, and with that he handed the jug to the boy. The boy tried to do like his grandpa did and smelled the jug first, and it smelled sweat and yet tart at the same time. He tilted the jug back and took a big gulp, and then he new what grandma meant when she said it smelled mellow but went down like fire. Grandpa made his cider out of one part fruit and two parts moon shine. He always said it was tasty and the boy had to agree, all though he was hard put to know what his grandpa was talking about. The boy handed the jug back to grandpa and it was then that the cider hit his gut. He felt this feeling of warmth spread all over him and he swore latter that if it had been twenty below out side he would have melted it just walking back to the house.

160

The three stayed out there taking turn about at the jug till grandma called them to dinner. When they got in side grandpa was weaving a little and leeanna's dad was walking real stiff and trying to keep a straight face, the boy was all over the place. Some how he couldn't make his feet behave and they kept trying to go in different directions at the same time, and he thought this was funny and kept laughing about it. Grandma got them all to the table and set them down. Grandpa stumbled through the prayer and finely gave up and just said God thank you for everything, and grandma said you mean for your hard cider, and then ever one got quiet and then the boy belched and ever one started to laugh, The meal went off with out a hitch and after it was over ever one stretched out and took a nap. About five they all got up and ate leftovers and while they were doing this it started to snow again, and it was one of those soft wet snow's. The whole tribe looked out at it and then grandpa bowed his head and with a soft low voice said God thank you for this day and all who are here. Grandma put her head against his shoulder and sighed a small sigh.

The snow was to deep for leeanna and her dad to leave that evening so they spent the night and grandpa and Leeann's dad stayed up talking about one thing then another. Leeanna and the boy and grandma cleaned up the kitchen then set about getting beds ready for them to sleep. Leeanna told the boy she could not remember when she had, had a better time and the boy said he felt the same, and just as ever one was getting ready for bed leeanna reached up when know one was looking and kissed the boy on the lips. This shook him clear to his toes, and he felt things he had never felt before, and was hard put to under stand it but made up his mind to talk with grandpa as soon as possible. So ended November, and it left memory's that would be carried all the rest of there life's.

A week latter the boy was in town when he saw Leeanna down at the drug store, she asked him what he was doing in town and he said he was there with his grandpa and that his grandpa was seeing a man down at the feed store. She asked how long his grandpa would be and he said about two or three hours depending on how many lies that were telling each other. Leeanna asked him if he would like to have lunch with her and her dad, and the boy just beamed and said he would, and then followed her home.

When Grandpa caught up with him he looked sad and scared. He said grandma was sick and that he was going to have to take her to the hospital. The boy told him he was having lunch with Leeanna and her dad and his grandpa said that was good and then he left.

The boy pushed the thought of grandma being sick out of his head.. She would get well and then everything would be all right. For now he had a lunch to go to. He would regret this for the rest of his life.

23

Leeanna's dad had on a pair of blue jeans and a plaid shirt. He wore cowboy boots and looked all big and warm. The boy hit them with one question after another and they were hard put to keep up with him. He finely came down from the clouds and told them that the meal all laid out for them would make the rooster crow. Her dad took them in to the kitchen and set them down. He poured Leeann a glass of butter milk fresh from the cow. While he was drinking it down he went in and brought out the ham. He was setting thing's on the table enough for a convention and it was only when leeanna said that she was afraid the table might break that he slowed down.

The boy was so happy to have some folks around he could hardly contain his self. He finely held the seat out for leeanna to set down and then he set down next to her. He looked at her dad asked him if he would please do the honors of blessing the food and he, said he would. They all bowed there head's and held hands for the prayer.

Once the saying of grace was over, leeanna said she would do the honors of dishing out the food. The Boy and her dad was only to happy to let her do it. She filled there plates and then filled her own, and set down. The three of them dug in like starved pig's and it wasn't soon till the food started to diminish at a rapid rate.

After lunch the three of them went into the living room and set down for some talk and coffee. As the day wore on and it was getting along toward night fall then Leeanna's dad turned on the radio to catch some of the late evening programs. He tuned it till he got some Christmas music.

The three of them set and listened to the music for a while then leeanna's dad said they had to get going. The boy had been dreading that statement, but knew that they had to go. He told them that he was real happy that he had come out and that they should come out more and see him soon.. He shook hands with the man and he went out through the door. He turned toward Leeanna and was about to shake her hand to when she came into his arm's and planted a kiss right on his lip's. He looked surprised, but only for a second then he kissed her back and soundly at that. When they finely came up for air the boy felt all shaky in side, and the girl was breathing real hard and he could see her chest, such as it was, rising and falling. They looked at one another for a second or two then Leeanna said she loved him and always would. Before he could say anything she was out the door and in her dad's car with the door shut. He walked out side and watched them go. The next day his grandpa came home, and the news's he had was what the boy had been dreading.

24

Grandma had died in her sleep. Grandpa found the boy down at the milk house going about his chores and he felt like the whole world had caved in on him. He knew he had to tell the boy about it but he didn't know just how to do it. In a way he wanted to run to the hill's and just lay low till all these feeling's had left him behind, but he knew he couldn't do that, so he had decided to make the best of it and just lay it on the line, and hope all the pieces fell in place like they should.

He walked in on the boy as he was finishing up his milking and he leaned up against the stall the boy was working in. he asked him how thing's had been going and after he got his answer he just stood and stared at the wall. The boy knew something bad was wrong, but he couldn't bring himself to ask the question. He already knew the answer. The night before he had, had a dream. He had seen his grandma all dressed out in blue silk, and she was smiling and looked peaceful. He knew she had gone on to the other side and he was content to know she had with out having to be told about it. Soon grandpa looked down at the floor and then looked back up at the boy and the boy saw tear's in his eyes. Grandpa tried to brush them away but they kept coming. The boy walked over and put his hand in his grandpa's hand and just stood there with him for the longest time. Finely his grandpa said that maybe they should go to the house and see about something to eat, and the boy said he reckoned so.

When they got to the house the boy went in and started to set the table while his grandpa went and changed his clothes. They finely set down to eat and they ate in silence. The boy looked up at his grandpa a time or two and even started to speak but some how the words just wouldn't come, so he set there in silent pain and then the tear's stated to fall and it seemed as if they would never dry up. He felt like a broken water works. His grandpa didn't seem to notice, and it was some time till they got up from the table and went to there separate rooms.

The next morning at breakfast grandpa told the boy that they had to go into town to get the funeral arrangements made, and the boy said he would like to pass on it and stay at home and do the chores but his grandpa told him that he needed his help in picking out a casket and the type of gown that was to go on grandma so the boy said he would go along but sure wished that this was one trip that he could pass on, and grandpa said he felt the same but it had to be done so the best way was to just hold your head up and get along with it as best as they could.

They got into town about nine or a little after and went straight to the Doug's funeral home. When they walked in through the door's there was a tall skinny man in a black tight fitting coat and his hair was combed back and held down with some kind of grease. The boy thought he looked like death him self and felt sure that he was the angle of death in person. He got behind his grandpa and tried to hide from the man. The man told grandpa that the remains were in the back and asked him what he wanted him to do with the deceased. Grandpa said he wanted to pick out a casket and then see to some kind of clothes for her to wear and the man said that he could show him just about anything he wanted to see and turned around and walked through a curtain that was behind him. Grandpa and the boy just stood there. Grandpa looked at the boy and the boy saw his Adam's apple bob up and down a time or two then grandpa set off for the curtain and what ever lay behind it. The boy was right on his heels. When they got through to the other side the boy felt like maybe he was going to cash in his chip's and just get it all over with cause this just seemed to be to hard a thing for him to have to do and he could only guess at how his grandpa was feeling and in truth he didn't really want to know, as his feeling's were enough to do him in and he felt that any thing more would just be more then he could stand.

The man took them over to where a bunch of long boxes were setting on saw horses and said that if grandpa couldn't find something that suited him here that he had more in the basement. Grandpa looked them all over for a few minutes and then he walked over to one that was bronze with golden angles on the corners. The inside was all white with satin. There was a pillow in it. Grandpa walked up and put his hand on it and then looked at the boy and the boy shook his head up and down a time or two so grandpa turned to the man and said that he would be taking this one. The man said fine that it was a casket to last the age's, and grandpa said now he wanted to see the cloth's. the man took them to another room and showed them some gowns and grandpa picked out a blue one that was about the prettiest thing that the boy had ever seen. It was silk and the boy had never seen any thing like it in his life, and felt that the only time you wore it was when they put you away. He made up his mind to stay as far away from silk as long as he lived.

While the boy was worrying this over in his mind the man and grandpa were getting some paper's signed and making thing's all proper and legal. As they started to leave the man said that the deceased would be ready for viewing in a few days and grandpa asked when the funeral would be and the man said Saturday and grandpa said that would be fine, then he and the boy left.

On the way to the car they ran into the fat lady that had come out to help the boy with milking and the boy spoke to her. She just kind of snorted through her nose and with a flip of her butt set off down the street. Grandpa asked him what that was all about and he told him and he grandpa laughed a little. The boy told him that it was good to here him laugh again and his grandpa said that hard time and hurt had a way of healing it's self with time and that what they needed to do now was to get on with there lives as best as they could. The boy agreed.

25

The Saturday of the funeral was a dreary day. The clouds had come up out of the west and there was a hint of rain in the air. Grandpa got up early and was in the process of getting dressed when he heard the boy moving around in his perch. Grandpa set on the side of the bed for what seemed like a year or more to him, then he got up and went to get his Sunday suit on. He had only worn this suit three time's in his life and in truth he didn't want to wear it now, but felt that it wouldn't be proper to dress any other way.

The boy in the mean time was getting dressed. His grandpa got him a suit and he was hard put to get into it. It was a three piece affair, and it had a vest and everything. The boy got into his white shirt and his black pant's. He had to put on socks and they were something else. He finely managed to get them on, then came the shoes. They were real stump jumper's. they were black and had a band running across the top. He was use to wearing moccasins, and was hard put to wear them, but made up his mind to do it, after all if grandpa could get spruced up and like it, so could he.

At breakfast grandpa was quite and down cast. The boy set in on his corn bread and milk, but grandpa just set and stared at his plate and didn't eat a thing. The boy had noticed that ever since grandma had passed over that his eating was down, but he figured that it would pick up after a while. Grandpa finely spoke up and said that he guessed that they had better be getting on into town so they could plant ma and be done with it, the boy said he guessed so, so they set out for town. Half way there grandpa got choked up and couldn't seem to see the road. The boy reached over and put his hand on his right arm and just held it for a moment or two, and finely grandpa got his self calmed down and was able to see where he was going.

When they got into town and pulled up behind Doug's funeral parlor and got parked his grandpa set for a few minutes and got him self pulled together. They got out and went in and found some seats up front by the casket and set down. The man that had showed them around was there and he was going about the seating of the rest of the folks as they came in. After about fifteen minutes the place was packed full of friends and family that had come from near and far for the funeral. Grandpa said it looked like a family reunion, only grimmer, and the boy said if this is what a reunion is like he would just as soon pass on them and his grandpa said he felt the same way, but that the services had to be conducted and done right or else grandma couldn't rest in peace and if there was one thing he didn't want to happen was for her not to rest in peace cause sure as water is wet if she didn't when he went to join her she would give him the jigger fits for not seeing that her funeral was done right and proper, and he couldn't see spending the next thousand years or so being nagged at.

Soon the preacher got up in front and held his hands up for to stop the whispering and nose blowing. He stood there for a second or two then swelled him self up like a toad and started to talk. He told about how grandma was a fine christen and how she had helped others when ever she could. He got to leaning from one side of the podium to the other. He said she was an angle and that she had never done a mean thing in her life, and then he got wound up and set in on how fair minded she was and how she was one of the finest people he had ever met. The boy listened for a few minutes and then he started to looking around the room. He could see several people there that his grandma, if she didn't hate them, well she sure didn't like them, and it seemed that they were the one's shaking there heads up and down the most, and agreeing with what the wind bag was spouting out. The boy felt that he was going to be sick to his stomach.

It took the preacher about thirty minutes to finely wined down and when he was done he was sweating like a farm hand and all out of breath, and so was most of the people that had been listening to him. The ladies all had fans and they were beating the air fit to kill and the boy felt sure that if they kept it up much longer that there was going to be a twister right there in that room but after a while the folks all lined up and started to make there pass by the casket. Some of the women would stop and bow there heads and then give a little shake of there shoulders and then dab at there eyes a few times and then move on so's the one behind them could come up and do the same thing. There was so much crying going on that the boy felt sure that if they wrung out all there hankies that they would have a whole wash tub full of water.

By and by they all walked out and started to getting in there cars for the trip to the grave yard. Grandpa and the boy was to ride with director Mr. Doug's and the rest of the tribe was going to follow along in there car's. Grandma went out first in the hearse, and then came grandpa and the boy and behind them the rest of the folks. It took about ten minutes or so to get to the grave yard and when they did get there most of the cars couldn't fit in so some of the people ended up parking on the high way and along side the ditch. This made for some bad times for the folks driving by and in the end there was a bad car crash cause of the man driving by was rubber necking and not paying attention where he was going.

The hearse pulled up at the grave site and stopped. Next came Doug's with grandpa and the boy. He pulled to a stop behind the hearse and told grandpa and the boy to get out. The pall bears were behind the hearse and were waiting for Doug's to open the back. It was a real solemn time for ever one. Doug's walked around with his hands behind his back and directed everything with a jerk of his head, and the pall bears lined up three to each side and started to pull the casket out of the hearse, Grandpa and the boy were to have places at the grave side and the rest of the folks just took up station where ever they could. The casket was finely place over the grave and the pall bears were each holding a rope and looking a t Doug's for the finely nod of his head. The preacher got out or his car and walked to the head of the grave and held his bible and looked real thoughtful for a minute or two then he said for ever one to bow there heads and said a prayer that seemed to go on for ever, and when he finely finished it had started to rain. It was a soft rain at first then there was a crack of lighting and then it was like some one had opened the flood gate's of heaven and the rain came down like there was no tomorrow. Doug's looked up at the sky, then with a nod of his head the pall bears let grandma down into the cold damp grave. Doug's then asked grandpa if he would like to put in a hand full of dirt and grandpa stepped forward and bent down and took up a hand full of dirt and walked over and dropped it in on top of the gasket, then he said, "It says in the good book that where your treasure lye's, there your heart lye's also, well now... you've just put my treasure in the ground, so I leave my heart here with her." He then turned around and walked to the car and got inside.

The boy walked up behind him and threw some dirt into the grave and then he beat a fast exit for the car as well. The rest of the folks were hard put to see what was going on due to the rain but the one's in front relayed the events back to the one's that couldn't see and told all that was going on.

The services were over and ever one was going to meet at grandpa's house for the after dinner services. Grandpa told the boy that he would just as soon go to the dog's rather then put up with a bunch of talk and the likes, but the boy reminded him that grandma would of wanted it that way so he relented and said if ma would of wanted it like that then he guessed he could go along with some more of the foolishness, but he was hard put to see why the people didn't just go along and let him alone, so he could deal with his grief and be done with it, but the boy said maybe it was there way of dealing with there's also, and grandpa said maybe so, and then he felt better cause he might be helping some one else.

The after services affair was a pizon long thing, and the boy and his grandpa didn't think that the people would ever get out and go home, but after three or four hours the last of them left and the place got quite once again, Grandpa said if one more person was to walk up to him and pat him on the shoulder and shake there head he might just explode and do some bodily harm and then some, and the boy said he felt the same way.

They set around the house for the better part of the afternoon, till the bawling of the cow's came to there ears and then they got up and went down to the milk house and started in on the milking. While they were milking the boy said that cows were just plain old indifferent to what people felt, and his grandpa said that was so, and that all a cow knew was that when they were hungry they ate, and when there utters were full they wanted to be milked and that when they needed to shit or piss they did that too. The boy said maybe being a cow would be better then being a human, and his grandpa said maybe so in some way's but he still felt that being a human with all the faults was better then being a dump animal.

That night the boy had a dream. He was standing in a long valley and there were all kind of animals standing around. There were rabbits and deer. There were bears and lions and cows. There was some chickens and doves and all kinds of birds, The place was pure and simple. The clouds were high and the looked all soft and fluffy, like they do in Oklahoma in the summer time. The boy was standing in the middle of all of this when he heard a voice, and by damn it was his grandma's voice he was hearing. She told him that she would always be with him and that he must always do right and not cross the law. She told him that he would have a hard time of it in the future but that he would come through it ok. She said she loved him and that she would always be with him, even when he felt like he was alone, she would be there.

He woke straight up in bed and was calling her name when he came to him self. He looked all around the room and then got down and looked under the bed. Man that was some dream he thought and then he got back into

the bed and lay there thinking about the dream for the
rest of the night. At breakfast he told his grandpa about
the dream and his grandpa said he had, had one to, and
it was almost the same one. The two of them just set
in silence and thought about what had gone on. Finely
grandpa said that grandma was with them and it was her
way of letting them know that she was around and that
they had better watch there :P's and Q's, or else she would
get them for sure. This made the boy uncomfterable. The
thought of having grandma around and him not being
able to see her was almost to much for him to bare. He
thought he would never get undressed again as long as she
was around and watching and when he told his grandpa
how he felt his grandpa just laughed and said that even
if she saw him she wouldn't be upset, cause she had seen
naked men before in her life, so it wouldn't be anything
new to her. The boy said it wasn't about her being upset,
he said he was worried about his self being upset. His
grandpa laughed even harder and told him to just get on
with living and to let him worry about the rest. With this
statement grandpa got up and left the room. As he walked
out the boy could see his shoulders shaking and knew he
was laughing under his breath.

26

Summer time and the living is easy, fish are jumping' and the cotton is high. Your daddy's rich and your ma is good looking, so hush now baby don't you cry. This song was on the radio when the boy turned it on. It was two week's to the day that they had put grandma away, and the boy was feeling down. The weather had gotten worse and it was snowing out side. The boy listened to the song and wished It was summer time and that all the trouble he had in his life would just up and go away, but he knew that it didn't work like that, and that he would have to go on with the mess of living even if he didn't want to. Grandpa had gotten so he couldn't eat. Ever thing he ate came back up and he was starting to look like a starved gentile, to use the boys words. He had tried to talk with his grandpa about his not eating but all he would say was that he wasn't hungry and to let him alone, that he would eat when he got good and ready and not one second sooner.

That night as they were coming back from the milk barn, grandpa looked at the sky and said well now.... would you look at that. The boy stopped and turned to look at what his grandpa was pointing at. The moon was full and around the out side of it was a bright glowing ring. Grandpa called it a winter's moon. He said that if you was to count the stars in side the ring that how ever many that it was, then you would know when it was going to snow next. There were three stars in side the ring and grandpa said that in three days that they would have a snow that would do in the banker's and all the rest of the crooks that lived.

It was almost three days to the minute when it started to snow. It came down like cotton and stuck to the ground like a poor brother in law sticks to his sister, it got cold. Colder then the boy could ever remember it getting. Grandpa said it was so cold that the people in hell was asking for blankets. The boy said that the chickens were all setting on one nest and that they were taking bids on who would lay the first egg and then who would set on it. Grandpa said that he had seen it colder but he couldn't remember when and then he said that if ma was alive she could tell about it. The boy asked if it was colder then when he met the cold maker, and his grandpa said it was and that before it was over that it would get colder. He went on to say that when you had a winter's moon that there was no holding back the weather and that the cold maker was out and running and that there was nothing on the face of the earth that could stop it.

That night when the boy went to bed he could here the wind kicking up around the eve's and he said a silent prayer that God would watch over him and his grandpa and not let any thing happen to them. He fell asleep then and didn't wake up till the sun was peaking it's head over the eastern part of the world. The first thing he heard was a rooster crowing and just in general telling the world about how he was the best at what ever it was he could do. The boy got up and went down stairs and into the kitchen. He fixed him self a glass of butter milk and got some corn bread. He put some butter on the bread and then stuck it on top of the old cook stove. He waited till the butter melted and watched it run into the corn bread. This was eating in style as far as he was concerned. He then took his meal and went into the dinning room and set down. He had been eating for a few minutes when he realized that his grandpa was late getting out of bed. He went into the front room and looked about.

Grandpa wasn't there. He then went to look in the bathroom. Nope he wasn't there either. He then went into grandpa's bed room. There he lay. His eyes were open and he wasn't breathing. The boy knew he was dead just by looking at him.

27

The boy looked at his grandpa and for the first time in his life he felt lost. It wasn't at all like he had felt the time he was lost in the woods. It was a feeling of being with out. He felt that there was know one on the face of the earth that could help him. He set down on the side of the bed and held his head in his hands. He knew he would have to get hold of some one to take care of grandpa but he felt just to tired to do it. He could here the cows in the back ground and they were bawling to be milked, and he knew that he would have to go on, but life just seemed to hard for him just at this moment. He set there and then the tears started to come. He had lost both his grandparents in less then a month and he was hard put to know what to do.

After thirty minutes of so the boy stood up and wiped his eyes dry. He went down to the milk house and got the milking out of the way. After he got the milk in the cooler he set out for whities house. His mom and dad had gotten a phone and he knew he would have to call the sheriff and the funeral home. It seemed to him that the funeral home was making a killing off of his folks and he knew he would have to deal with Doug's and his bunch. But that was just the way it was and he knew he would have to go through the whole business of putting grandpa under the ground, but how was he to do it.? This was on his mind as he walked up into whities drive way.

The boy knocked on the door and waited for some one to answer the door. he could here movement inside the house and soon the door opened and there stood whities mom. She looked at him for a minute then invited him into the house. He walked in and went over and set down in the chair by the wood stove. He just set there and didn't say anything. Whities mom walked over and stood over him. She reached down and tussled his hair with her right hand and then she asked him what it was she could do for him. Before he knew it the words were rushing out in a stream like a dam had broken.

Whities mom just listened to him and didn't say any thing. After he came up for air and was calmed down some and was wiping the tears away, she said she would make the phone calls and for him not to worry none, that ever thing would be all right. She left to make the call and the boy set there in silent misery. She was gone a long time but finely came back and when she did she had some milk and cake. She gave it to the boy and told him to relax for a few minutes. He asked her who she had called and she said Doug's funeral as well as the high sheriff. The boy said he would start for home soon as he had finished up his cake, but she said he was to wait here till the sheriff came to get him. The boy set in abject silence then till the sheriff got there.

When the sheriff arrived he came to the door and knocked. As soon as whities mom opened the door he came in and told the boy in a soft voice that they had to go along to his home to take care of a few matters. They walked out and got in his car and set off down the road to ward's the boy's home. The boy didn't say a word all the way, and it was only when they were turning into his drive way that the sheriff spoke to him. He asked him how his grandpa had died, and the boy told him he had found him in his bed and his eyes were open and he could see that he wasn't breathing, so that is when he went to call for some help. The sheriff listened in silence, and only grunted when the boy had finished his tail.

About the time they pulled to a stop and was getting out into the drive turns Doug's and his hearse, but to the boy's surprise right behind him came his aunt. The one who had been told to stay away and leave him be. The boy got behind the sheriff and watched as her car came to a stop behind the hearse. She got out of the car and came stomping up to the sheriff and demanded that he do something about her losing her dad. Now the boy caught the squint of the sheriff's eye and knew she had said the wrong thing. Ever one knew you asked the sheriff to do something and didn't demand any thing of him, cause sure as water is wet he might just cloud up and rain all over you. The high sheriff stood there for a second, and the boy could see his right hand shaking, and the squint had gotten to almost deep stare. The boy knew his aunt was in for ol'ned for sure, but then the high sheriff took a deep breath and let it out real slow between his teeth and the boy could hear the sound it made and then the sheriff said he was doing all he could, but that if she wanted to know who it was who passed her pa over to the other side, she would have to take that up a higher power then him, namely **god**, and with that he turned on his heel and in doing so almost knocked the boy for a roll of Sunday's. When his aunt saw the boy she made as if she was going to go for him but the high sheriff grabbed her arm and told her to pull her horns in or she just might get them clipped. She glared first at the boy, and then at the sheriff, she then set off down the walk towards the front door.

As she was going through the door Doug's was coming out and he didn't see her, so he almost ran over her, or at least grandpa did cause he was on a roll away bed and Doug's had a fair head of steam when he hit the front door with the end of the bed. The aunt got caught right across the middle with the edge of the bed end and it folded her up right on top of grandpa. She jumped off the top of grandpa and ever one could see she was winded, meaning her breath had been knocked out of her. When she got her air back she gave Doug's a cussing that would pin back the ears of a tent preacher three canyon's away. When she finely finished up with a general cussing of the whole male population of the human race, she then turned and walked with the stiff dignity of a person who has just been made the butt of a bad joke. As she was driving down the drive the high sheriff said that if he had to be married to her he would just pack up and move to the north pole and mate with polar bear's. The boy said he didn't blame him and in the long run it might be safer. Doug's just shook his head in agreement.

Doug's took grandpa into town and the boy rode in with the high sheriff. When they got to the funeral home, the boy asked Doug's how he was supposed to go about getting his grandpa put away, but Doug's said that his grandpa had already taken care of that, and that all the boy need do was to sign that it was ok for him to start. The boy asked where he was to sign, and Doug's showed him. Doug's then asked the boy to pick out the putting away clothes and said they had already been paid for also, so the boy went in and picked out a white silk shirt, with a string tie. Next came a cow man's vest and a black coat, The pant's were black when he asked about shoes or boot's Doug's told him that they didn't put people away with them on, but the boy said he would like them put on his grandpa any way, so Doug's told him he would do it but it would cause a lot of fuss and bother, but the boy said his grandpa had paid for the whole works and by golly he was going to get it. Doug's just nodded his head ok. The boy then asked to see the casket and Doug's said he had already picked one out and then showed the boy one that looked just like the one that grandma had been put away in. The boy said that it was a right nice casket and he was glad that his grandpa would be resting in peace in comfort. The boy then turned and left and walked out side. The day was just about gone and he was looking at a long walk home when he saw the high sheriff standing there next to his car. He walked over to him to see if maybe he could take him back to the house and he said he had been waiting for that very thing. The boy got in as well as the sheriff and they set out for home once again.

On the way the sheriff said that while the boy had been inside with Doug's his aunt had caught up with him and had told him that as soon as the funeral was over that she would be taking full possession of the farm and for him to tell the rat, meaning the boy, to be off the place the day after the funeral or she would see to it that he was sent to a reform school. The boy asked him if she could do that and the high sheriff said that with her being the oldest living relative, and being the processor of the will that she could do just about anything that she wanted to do, The boy next asked how much time he had and the sheriff said about three or maybe four days, and the boy said that, that would be more then enough time to do what he had to do. The high sheriff started to ask what it was he was going to do, then thought better of it, and it was only latter that he remembered back to this talk and was glad he had kept his mouth shut and didn't have to lie.

It was coming on to full dark by the time that the sheriff had dropped him off at the mail box at the head of the drive leading to the house. He said he was going on down the road to see a man about a jug of moon that he was going to buy, the he asked the boy not to tell on him and the boy told him not to worry that his grandpa had sometimes sampled the shine and he didn't see any thing wrong with it, and the sheriff said he wished that ever one was like the boy, and went on to say that it would sure make his job easier if they were. He then said good by and drove off.

The boy walked to the house and the closer he got to it the worse he felt. It seemed to him that the farm was not the same and never would be again. He walked in the door and went into the kitchen. He fired up the old cook stove and set the coffee pot on it to heat up the morning brew, and then he went down to the smoke house and got him self a slab of ham. By the time he was back in the kitchen the coffee was starting to boil and he set it off the side to cool a might before he poured in some cool water to settle the grounds. He then sliced the ham in strips and made him self a sandwich. He poured him self some coffee and then took the whole mess up to his perch. He lit his lamp and started to sort through his thing's to decide what he was going to keep and what he was going to take.

He got out and old brown cardboard suit case and opened it up and set it on his bed. He then started to lay in his thing's that he would be keeping. He put in his shirts, there were three of them, next came his pant's. He packed two pair and he would be wearing one pair, He kept his suit out for the funeral along with the shoes and socks, but knew just as soon as the funeral was over he would leave them here in his perch. He was starting to think that the suit had something to do with dying and he was going to be rid of it as soon as he could. Next he put in his 22 rifle, but only after he had taken it apart and wrapped it in a pillow case. He put it in along with his shells. Next came his under wear. Then he closed the lid and wrapped a belt around it and pulled it tight to keep the lid closed. He then went down to where grandpa had kept the house money. His grandpa had told him that there was about six hundred dollars in the sock and it was to be used only if need be. The boy took it and placed it under a can in the well house. He then went to do his chores down at the milk barn. After the milking was done and the milk was put away he went back to the house and went to bed. Tomorrow would be a long and busy day.

He awoke just before day light and went down to the milk house to repeat the chores of the night before, and after he was done he set off down the road to talk some business with Mr. Highcorn. When he got to the Highcorn home he walked up and knocked on the door. Mr. Highcorn came to the door and when he saw who it was he came out and set down cross legged on the ground, and the boy did the same. At first they just set there and then the boy took out some tobacco and a pipe. He packed the pipe then took out a Lucifer and struck it on his pant's pocket and then lit the pipe. He took a couple of drags then passed it to Highcorn. Highcorn looked grave when he took the pipe and did like wise.

After the pipe had been offered to the sky the earth and the sun and the moon only did they then start to talk.

The boy let Highcorn speak first. He was older and wiser, and it was only respect to let him go first. Highcorn talked about his grandparents but only in the past tense, as ever one knew it was bad to talk of a person as if they were dead cause it might bring he who takes life to your door, so they spoke as if his grandparents were still alive.

Highcorn spoke with respect about grandpa and his grandma. He spoke of him as a friend and brother. He spoke of grandma in soft tones and called her sister. When he had finished he held the pipe back to the sun moon earth and star's then handed it to the boy. The boy said that all he said was true and now he would like to know if he would be interested in helping his brother out by buying some of his cows ? Highcorn didn't wait for the pipe to be passed back to him, he just said one word, yes. The boy said he could pay what ever he felt would be a good and fair price and for him to come that after noon to make the bargain, Highcorn just grunted and nodded his head. The boy then re lit the pipe and he and Highcorn smoked it down to ashes then dumped the pipe out on the ground and then they both ground the toes of the right foot into it. Highcorn then went into his house and the boy went home to wait for him.

He didn't have long to wait. Highcorn showed up about and hour latter, and he had the sheriff with him. The sheriff said that if there was going to be a sale that he had to be in on it to make sure that ever thing went according to hoyl. The boy didn't know who hoyl was, but guessed he was some one else he would have to deal with at a latter date.

Highcorn walked over to where the boy had the cattle bunched in the holding pen, and then turned to the boy and said he would give him fifty dollars a piece for them the boy started to say sold, but the sheriff spoke up and said that he had gotten a lot more money from his settlement with the bankers when he lost his farm and then said that he was trying to cheat the boy, and it wasn't right. Highcorn looked a little put out but he didn't say anything back to the sheriff instead he stood hip shot with his right hand on his hip and then looked up out from under his straw hat and said ok, now about sixty dollars and the sheriff said well that's some better but still not good enough, and then went on to say how about a flat seventy five dollars a piece for the lot, and Highcorn looked at the boy to see if he agreed and when he saw he did, he said sold him self. The two of them shook hands and then Highcorn said he would have the check to him that after noon, but the sheriff said that cash money would be better so Highcorn said he would bring that instead, and then he turned around and left.

The sheriff waited till Highcorn was gone then he turned to the boy and said that he had made a good deal and then wanted to know what he was going to do with the money, and the boy said it was for traveling, and the sheriff said for him to say know more that what he didn't know couldn't hurt him and then he left.

Highcorn came back that afternoon with his money and paid it out to the boy then he and his kin drove the cows out of the holding pen and down the road to his place. The boy then went to the well house and put his money in the sock with the money he had gotten from the house. After this was done he went back up to the house to fix him self some dinner, and he was in the process of eating it when he heard a car pull up in front of the house. He got up and went to see who it was. As he walked into the front room he saw through the window his aunts car and knew he was in for a rough time, then the thought came to him that his grandparents were dead and he didn't have to take any thing off her ever again if he didn't want to. He turned around and went to the side door going from the dinning room out side. He grabbed a sandwich and took his milk and went out through the door as she was banging on the front. He went down by the cellar and around the hog pen and through the garden to the well house. It took longer that way but he couldn't be seen from the house while getting to the well house. In the distance he heard a window break and knew that his aunt had broken the window out of the front door so she could snake her hand in to unlock the door. He waited till she was in the house before he went into the well house. it only took a second to get the sock with the money and get back out side, but even as he was doing this he could here her in the distance calling him a bastered, and a little son of a bitch and trying to get him to come out from where ever he was hiding. He smiled to him self cause he knew she would never find him in a million years, and with that he went on down to the barn and put a saddle on the horse. He had just climbed into the saddle and started out toward the pasture when he heard the side door bang open and then his aunt screaming for him to come to her or she would kill him if she had to find him. He didn't even look back, and as he rode her voice got fainter and fainter, till he could only here the wind blowing against his ears and the sound the saddle made when he shifted his weight and the sound of the horse hoof's as it hit the grass.

He rode to the back of the pasture and then cut the fence that would let him through to the next mile section. He didn't bother to repair the fence cause he knew there were know cattle grazing in the field's and his grandpa's had all been sold so there was know reason to repair it and he just rode on, He went down behind whities house and then turned back toward the east and finely made his way to the bottoms. He would be safe here for a while, but knew he would have to be pushing on as soon as he could. He went to his saddle bags and got out some dried beef, what some call jerky, and ate some. He then staked out the horse, and rolled him self up in his coat and went to sleep.

28

The next day came on cloudy and cold, and he awoke to a frosty chill in the air. He got some making's together and started a fire. While the coffee was making he went to his horse to see how he was doing. He found him a little worse for the wear due to the fact the horse had spent more then his fair share of time under the roof of the barn, and eating hay and what not. He rubbed him down and then got him saddled. He went back to his fire and poured him self a cup of coffee and ate some more dried beef.

He got into the saddle and started the tired old horse forward. He knew that the horse was going to give out soon, but he wanted to get as far down the road as he could before he did. He went deeper into the bottoms and finely found him self a camp where he could set for awhile. There was one thing he wanted to do before he left the country, and that was he wanted to see grandpa put away, after that the whole bunch could go to the dogs. The funeral would be tomorrow, and he was going to it or know the reason why. Oh he wouldn't be there among the people to see grandpa put to rest, but he would be around to watch, even if it was at a distance, but that was better then nothing the way he saw it.

The day seemed to fly by and the night was much the same, so when the day broke it was to see him on the horse and heading for the grave yard. He got to the grave yard about ten, and tied his horse up in a thicket about a mile away. He then made his way to the out skirts of the grave yard and settled down to wait. It was going on to noon when he saw in the distance the funeral procession. It was just like when they had put grandma away. Here come the hearse, then the family and then the folks behind to all say good by.

The hearse pulled up to the grave and stopped and Doug's got out and went to the family car. The only one to get out was the aunt that had wanted to do him in. He watched as they got grandpa onto the ground beside the grave then ever one stood back and the preacher came forward and made his pitch to the folks and it was longer and winder then before and as far as the boy was concerned grandpa was the only one who had it made in the bunch. After the ice age came and went the preacher finely shut up and the people all breathed a sigh of relief, the Paul bears came forward and lifted grandpa up and then set him into the grave. then his aunt came forward and took up a chunk of dirt and dropped it in on top of the casket and turned and walked back to the car and got in.

The rest of the folks all walked by and said there good by's, and then one by one they all left. Finely it was just the grave digger's left and they set in and got the grave filled up and then they to left. The boy waited a hour after ever one had gone before he went to where grandpa lay resting and then he stopped and bowed his head and said a prayer. After standing there for a few minutes he turned and went back to his horse and mounted. He took one more look at the grave yard and then turned the horse and rode him west toward the setting sun. That night found him just to the other side of Sapulpa and going down route 66 toward Oklahoma City. He was fair on his way and could only wonder at what all was going on back at the old home place.

He would have been shocked at what all was going on. His aunt had gone to the high sheriff and gotten a warrant for his arrest, and then had gone to the news paper and printed a description of him and even gave them a old school picture of him. She said that he was thief and that he was more then likely armed and that he should be shot on sight. There were people looking all over for him, especially since she had put out a hundred dollar reward for him.

It was a good thing he didn't know cause if he had he would have died laughing, and in truth the high sheriff wasn't looking to hard for him, and most of the people who knew him weren't either. There were a few who needed the money and they were looking real hard, but the sheriff knew they would never find him. He already knew he was gone, and that they would be hard put to lay hands on him, and he wasn't to sure that if they caught him that he would do anything about it any way.

The boy was on the rode for about three days when one morning he awoke to find his old horse dead. The horse was about twenty years old and grandpa had kept him around mostly because he liked him, and for no other reason. Grandma had called him a hay burner but grandpa had held on to him any way. The boy walked over to the horse and looked at him for a second or two then he started to cut brush to cover him up. He didn't want the horse found to soon.

After he finished his chore of covering the horse he shouldered his suit case and started to walk. He went up to the rode he had been following and held out his hand with his right thumb stuck out. He was going on down the rode, and he guessed he would have to make it one way or the other, and he could here his grandpas voice saying to him that tomorrow was another day, and all you had to do was make it through this one to get it. That was what he was going to do, make it through this one, just for now, and let tomorrow take care of it's self, that would be good enough, and that is the way it should be.

Epilogue

Leeanna asked if that was the end of the story, and the man who had been leaning against the old well house looked at her and said that it was, but then she asked him what happened after that and he said she already knew, but she said she didn't, and wanted to know how he got to the city and all that went on till he met up with her again, and he said he would tell her latter, but that right now he hungry and he wanted to go get something to eat, so she said they could go get something to eat, but that he must promise to tell her latter the rest of the story, and he said well now..., I might sand I might not, hell you already know what happened, but she said she knew a little but not all, or at least not the way he was telling it now, so he said he would tell her latter, after they had eaten.

They walked back to the car and got in and as they were driving away the man looked into the rear view mirror and he would have sworn that he could see his grandparents standing in the front yard and waving at him.

The End.......
For Now.................